This book is dedicated to that special breed of people;
those who get things done.

Detonation

Re-birth of a City

Ray King

Clear Publications

First published in June 2006 by Clear Publications Limited.

ISBN 10 0-9552621-0-0
ISBN 13 978-0-9552621-0-4

Typeset by Prestset,
Coronation Business Centre,
Hard Ings Road, Keighley, BD21 3NE

Printed and bound in Great Britain by Creative Print and Design Group,
Saxon Way, Harmondsworth, Middlesex UB7 0LW

Clear Publications Limited
Lynfield House,
Lynwood Avenue,
Appleton,
Warrington WA4 5AN

Acknowledgements

THROUGHOUT the fascinating period covered by this book I was a staff journalist with the Manchester Evening News, and it is to that newspaper that I owe thanks for the opportunity to be a close observer of the recent history of Britain's second city. I was in fact hired by the late, great Brian Redhead when he was editor in the early 1970s; he loved Manchester and I hope he would have enjoyed this account of its dramatic rebirth from catastrophe.

But I was a mere observer, not a doer like many of the people who contributed to this story and gave me hours of their time as interviewees. What they did, and indeed are still doing, is remarkable. Special thanks are due to Graham Stringer MP, former leader of Manchester city council, his successor Richard Leese and to the city's Chief Executive, Sir Howard Bernstein. The book Manchester: Shaping the City, published by the city council and the Royal Institute of British Architects, was a valuable source of information with an admirable narrative written by Jane Price. I am indebted too to Frances Done, Ian Simpson, Pat Karney and Janine Watson for their valuable help.

I thank also Sir David Trippier, the former Minister for Manchester who held several key government posts during his time as Conservative MP for Rossendale and, as recalled in his own memoirs, Lend Me Your Ears, played an absolutely crucial part in laying the groundwork for Manchester's success. So too did Lord Heseltine, who, as Secretary of State for the Environment and later Deputy Prime Minister, conceived City Challenge which transformed Hulme and the task force which oversaw the post-bomb regeneration of the city centre. His autobiography, Life in the Jungle, offers a vivid account of Manchester's response.

Gracious assistance was received from Greater Manchester Police, particularly from former Chief Superintendent Peter Harris, Assistant Chief Constable Ian Seabridge, Pc Stuart Pizzey, Superintendent Simon Garvey and Amanda Coleman, deputy director of corporate communications.

I am particularly grateful to my former Manchester Evening News colleague and good friend Andrew Nott, without whose support this book would never have been written. It is his knowledge, via essential contacts as a crime correspondent, that provided much of the narrative surrounding the terror attack and the subsequent hunt for the bombers. His confidence in the project has seen it published.

Ray King
June 2006

Contents

Contents

PROLOGUE

By Sir David Wilmot, QPM DL,
Chief Constable of Greater Manchester Police –
July 1, 1992 to September 30, 2002.

THE Saturday Manchester exploded I was in London at the Trooping of the Colour and reflecting on the enormous security effort that had been mounted for this most public of occasions. It crossed my mind that even though Manchester was making a tremendous effort to rejuvenate itself, it was highly unlikely that any traditional national 'pomp and circumstance' event would routinely be performed in a provincial city. On the contrary, if you wanted something extraordinary you had to make it happen yourself; which was why Manchester's successive bids for Olympic and Commonwealth Games were monumental achievements. To be involved in the process generated pride and confidence in the ability of our area to deliver something special. We had a track record of sorts, especially in the sporting arena, and were preparing that very day the final touches for a European Championship game to be played at Old Trafford on the Sunday.

The warning came. Emergency procedures were activated. The detonation occurred. Thankfully, the vast majority of people escaped without serious physical injury. It was an eerie and unreal feeling walking around the sealed off and deserted city centre. The obvious damage was enormous and more serious structural problems would be identified later.

However, one was already beginning to hear of positive action - by the emergency services, in the initial response by the City of Manchester, the responses of the commercial sector in the devastated area, and those of volunteer groups, hospital staff, transport staff, the media and, of course, the public. The initial sense of shock quickly gave way to the spirit found in the Games bidding process - defeat was not contemplated and 'doable' was the only option.

The leadership displayed by the City of Manchester was, of course, fundamental to the positive process but the officials were ably assisted by the best brains in the area and the patient and sustained support of all involved.

The football game was played and was a significant success from Manchester's point of view. This was a major, international sporting event at a time when Manchester city centre was still sealed off, but it was also a signal of 'business as usual'. Out of this devastation there came a rising enthusiasm to grasp opportunities and if the unthinkable had been done to our area, what at the time was unimaginable would be achieved in its renaissance.

There is no doubt that the City's leadership, coupled with the extraordinary political skills that were exercised, capitalised on the spirit of co-operation and determination that had been found and displayed right across the board in our Games bidding process. It was and still is a tremendous experience to have witnessed the resuscitation, revival and development of our severely wounded city to the vibrant, world class environment that we now enjoy.

What follows is the story of that achievement.

David Wilmot.

Chapter One

Countdown

HE couldn't have known, but when Chief Inspector Ian Seabridge arrived for work at Manchester's Bootle Street police station, the countdown had already begun.

The Euro '96 soccer tournament was seven days old and there had been a spot of bother the previous weekend with drinkers watching the games on television in bars across Manchester city centre, so he had decided to come in an hour early.

England were playing their arch rivals Scotland that afternoon at Wembley – a rare event in recent times because of previous partisan crowd trouble - and there was a powder keg atmosphere. Supporters of both teams were going to be coming into the city centre to gather round the screens in the hundreds of bars and pubs in the centre's square mile. Already, not yet mid morning, it was a scorching hot June day. To further complicate matters, hundreds of Germans had also arrived in Manchester for their game due to be staged at Old Trafford the following day and as more and more beer was consumed in the glorious sunshine, there was every chance of trouble breaking out, serious trouble.

The police tactical planning for Euro '96 had been going on for more than six months and extra officers had been drafted into the city, but the Chief Inspector was still very conscious of the extreme 'tribal' nature of England-Scotland clashes and the extra risks such feelings created far beyond most football matches.

He reflected on the smart negotiations which had persuaded publicans to sell their liquid wares this day in harmless plastic glasses. As designated 'bronze' commander for the weekend, he was in operational control of the city's streets and could do without any unnecessary trouble.

Still in his jeans and casual clothes, he parked his car in the courtyard of the police station and walked towards his office, anticipating a busy day. But before he reached it an urgent voice from the Crime Management Unit, which monitors the day's activities, grabbed his attention. One glance at the centre screen of the bank of monitors told him that football had suddenly become the least of his worries.

Minutes earlier a man with an Irish accent had telephoned the Granada TV studios switchboard in Manchester and stated calmly that there was a vehicle bomb in the city which would go off in one hour. Similar calls were made between 9.38am and 9.50am to North Manchester General Hospital, Sky TV, Salford University and the Garda in Dublin. Such calls were not that unusual. For reasons beyond most people's understanding, some individuals get a kick out of causing pandemonium with hoax calls and TV and radio stations and newspaper offices receive them on a regular basis. But this one was unusual because the voice used a codeword, one known to Special Branch. The reason is simple. When a terrorist organisation wants to cause genuine mayhem but not necessarily kill or maim a large number of people, it informs the authorities of the danger to allow them to get the public away. The terrorist gets his message across but reduces the chance of mass murder which could turn some of his supporters against his cause. The use of a codeword ensures the authorities start acting immediately.

In the case of the IRA, the information they provided about bombs was usually not specific and it often took time to locate the problem and identify it. The codeword didn't remove the danger, it just improved the odds of doing something about it.

This time it was a little different. The caller was exact about where the bomb had been placed, the corner of Cannon Street and Corporation Street. CCTV quickly showed a six tonne red and white Ford Cargo van, its hazard lights flashing, illegally parked outside the Marks and Spencer store close to an overhead walkway that led shoppers into the Arndale Centre mall. On a Saturday this was the busiest part of the city centre. It was packed with people.

PC Stuart Pizzey, a specialist in crime prevention, had three months earlier attended a seminar presented by a senior officer in MI5 who had warned that the threat from the IRA of a major event was considered very high. While he was involved in the planning of the police operation to cope with Euro '96 he suggested that the possibility of a terrorist action should be taken very seriously.

"I was considered the doom and gloom merchant," he said. "Most people in the room threw scorn on the idea. They felt that with all the extra police activity the IRA would never have considered trying to plant a bomb in Manchester. That morning, the day of the Queen's Official Birthday and the Trooping of the Colour in London, when the warning came I looked at the codeword and recognised it as genuine, then I looked at the location and timing and knew immediately that it was for real.

"I told the sergeant who was with me, Mike Rawlings, what I thought and he said, 'Oh my Lord! If that van is full? Oh my Lord!'"

The Crime Management Unit went to 'Code Red', the highest security level.

Another colleague, Inspector David Comerford, despatched officers to check out the van which had been abandoned on yellow lines by two men wearing hooded jackets at 9.19am. A traffic warden had ticketed it within three minutes of it being parked and alerted the removal squad. Their job would be to jack it up, put it on a low loader and take it to the car pound. They were immediately told not to bother.

The first policeman on the scene, Pc Gary Hartley, looked in the cab and noticed wires running from the dashboard, through a hole and into the back. That, armed with what he had been told, was enough for him to report back that he had found the target vehicle. Fortunately for him, for the traffic warden and for hundreds of other people nearby, he didn't attempt to get inside to investigate further. Later, forensics experts found the components of what could have been a tremble trigger, a simple booby-trap system with a ball bearing on a plate which, if caused to roll, would trip the primer and explode the bomb. Had that have been rigged up, the act of clambering in might have been enough to set it off.

Around the van, hundreds of shoppers were making their way in and out of the Arndale Centre and the Marks and Spencer's store. Some were pressed against its doors in the throng, sliding along the side. The van shouldn't have been there, this was a no-parking zone for a good reason. It was a nuisance. Occasionally, as another shopper shoved against it, it moved just a fraction, but not much as the truck was, ominously, sitting very heavily on its axles. There were so many people so close together that Mr Seabridge was reminded of the final sequence in the movie Crocodile Dundee when the hero walked across the heads of commuters in New York's packed subway. Except this wasn't funny.

He continued to watch using urban traffic cameras; there was no dedicated security CCTV at the time.

Two women, one with a baby in a pram, the other attempting to marshal four young children, were amongst those pushed against the side of the vehicle while trying to struggle through the crowds spilling off the pavement. He could see their faces and his throat was suddenly very dry. If that was the bomb and if it went off now, the consequences, the guaranteed carnage, was almost unimaginable.

Seabridge's boss, Chief Superintendent Peter Harris, was also in the building. He would not normally be there at a weekend but had come in on his day off to deal with a few matters. He was also celebrating having that day been awarded the Queen's Police Medal for outstanding service. "I visited the Crime Management Unit around 10am," he recalled. "I was planning to walk to Marks and Spencer's to get my sandwiches and I remarked to the sergeant who was looking at his VDU that it was going to be a good day. 'Not if this goes off it won't,' he replied."

Harris, who had been on several anti-terrorist courses, including the 'Satan Force' course run by the Army which was about dealing with bombs, took command of the communications room while his Chief Inspector quickly donned his uniform, nearly falling over as he tried to get both feet into the same trouser leg in his haste, and headed out of the building in the company of a constable. As he stepped outside he noticed the first contingent of officers deployed specifically for the Euro '96 tournament pull up in a van and park outside the station. During the next 80 minutes they were to be the difference between life and death for hundreds if not thousands of people, all at this moment blissfully unaware that this was not just another sunny day.

Pc Pizzey had developed, in collaboration with stores across the city, a pager alert system as a method of passing on information about roaming gangs of thieves preying on shops and shoppers, and also had direct telephone lines to shops and offices at his fingertips. He started to work the phones. "Some people wanted to discuss what it was all about," he remembered. "I just told them there was no time for that and they had to evacuate, fast. I was using two phones at once, one dialling out and the other receiving queries about whether the threat was genuine."

The word started to spread and the van became the epicentre of the evacuation of 80,000 men, women and children. The first officers on the scene immediately began the awkward and painstaking task of trying to move people away from the immediate area. It was obviously going to take time and they had absolutely no way of knowing how much of that precious commodity they had. They were looking at what they knew was a ticking bomb, but they also knew they had to stay. Frustratingly, their initial efforts at dispersing the crowd were ignored, the shoppers continued to shop, the mothers still concentrated on their children, the office workers moved busily on to their next appointment, deliverymen moved their boxes. It was business as usual despite the sudden arrival of blue uniforms.

It is a known principle. When an alarm goes off in a building, or there is a call for an evacuation, it is often initially ignored. Then some people start to heed the warning and leave and others follow, then practically everyone does what they should have been doing several minutes earlier and a trickle becomes a torrent. People have difficulty in imagining a crisis before it has happened, sometimes until it is far too late. An extreme example occurred in Manchester in May 1979 when a fire broke out in the Woolworth's store in Piccadilly. As the flames began to spread from the furniture area a cashier started to cash up rather than run until she was ordered out by her boss. She lived. At the same time a 70-year-old customer in the dining area on the same floor irritably told an agitated assistant imploring him to leave that he was going to finish his soup. He was one of ten who died, asphyxiated in moments by choking fumes.

On this day, seventeen years later, one hairdresser refused to ask his customers to leave the salon on the grounds that they had chemicals in their hair and it was "too dangerous". In another salon an elderly lady refused to leave until her hair was rinsed. She was spirited away to a car wash in Cheetham Hill. A number of small shop owners were reluctant to leave their premises unattended and the manager of one larger store became actively obstructive because he viewed the evacuation merely as a loss of custom.

Several shoppers kept on insisting that they had to get to M&S because they had clothes they needed to take back or presents to buy for Father's Day, the following day. And a group of workmen refused to budge because they were on weekend double time.

"You've got to leave NOW. Please get back," was greeted with an initial reluctance because everybody thought what they were in the city centre for was important and bomb scares nearly always turned out to be just that; scares. However, the growing urgency in the officers' voices - plus the fact that they were all wringing wet with sweat – started to get the attention of the majority and people started, grudgingly, to move away.

One of the first on the scene, 32-year-old Sergeant Philip Naughton said, "Getting killed isn't in the job description for the police. There was the option for any of us to pack it in, go home and turn up at the Job Centre on Monday, but on the day, at that time, it simply didn't occur to any of us."

Pc Vanessa Winstanley added: "I was trying to stress to people that the bomb threat was real, that we knew it wasn't a hoax, but they ignored me.

There were all kinds of excuses such as they had to get their car because it was on double yellow lines and they didn't want a ticket. Someone insisted that they had to get a book for the weekend."

Pc Wendy McCormick ran into Marks and Spencer's to raise the alarm and then started evacuating other shops and restaurants. People were slow to move," she said. "I remember thinking I don't want to die because someone wants to finish their pizza."

By now, having had a closer look at the six tonner, the police thought they were probably dealing with a large device – a small one could have been delivered by car – however, no-one could have guessed that the 3,300 lbs of home-made explosives was about to become the largest bomb ever to explode in peacetime on the UK mainland.

The massive departure gained momentum and gathered speed. Some people started to walk quickly, more urgently, as the idea of what might be about to happen took root in the minds of those who had a few minutes earlier been concentrating on other matters. Suddenly it was going to be perfectly all right to return that dress to M&S next week. A bit of overtime could always be made up. Even the risk of orange hair paled into insignificance. The word was spreading. From the air the crowd appeared like a circular, expanding ripple in water caused by a fallen stone. But the wave of people was still moving slowly, and no-one knew when the clock would stop.

Harris glanced at his watch, then up at the clock on the wall to confirm. The hour was nearly up and there were still far too many people far too close. He tried to look calm but his heart was racing.

"I kept telling myself it won't go off" he said. "That's what you think, that's what's supposed to happen. You get the warning, you deal with the situation, the IRA gets its publicity and everyone goes home. But I knew time was short."

While one group of officers pushed people out from the epicentre, several more were working to keep people out of the continuously expanding cordon. Without the football extras it would simply not have been possible.

"We would not have had the manpower to move that many people as far back as we did without them," Mr Seabridge freely admitted. "As it was we were using security guards from shops to help out. It was a desperate race against time but, of course, we had no idea how much of that was left.

Away from the epicentre, many people convinced themselves they were safe whether or not there was a bomb in Corporation Street as long as they were around the corner, unable to see the van, out of the line of any blast. They figured that if there was an explosion they would be shielded by the other buildings. They were wrong.

Seabridge did a double take as he walked past STA Travel on Deansgate which had large glass windows at both its main frontage and its rear entrance. The ten staff were still working at their terminals, blithely discussing holidays with want-away students.

"Let's just say my instructions were abrupt and unequivocal and they all made their own immediate departures," he said.

The Army bomb squad arrived after hurtling down the M62 from its base in Liverpool and took up a position near Sam's Chop House, just off Cross Street, 200 yards from the van. They quickly deployed a 'Pigstick disrupter' to engage the suspect vehicle. The device is essentially a gun which can fire a number of different rounds of ammunition or explosive charges, each with a different and very specific capability. They are designed to deal with package bombs or car bombs where the explosive is behind a thin skin, be it plastic, cardboard, or in this case, the thin metal of a van. One round opens the package to reveal the bomb and its primer and a second round disables the core of the bomb without – most of the time – setting it off. It is mounted on a robot vehicle with a video camera attached so that the Army specialist can locate the exact position of the primer, identify its type and set his machine accordingly.

The soldier sent it on its way. Harris knew that the hour deadline had now passed. He glanced again at his clock. When the clock in the lorry clicked down to zero, its Semtex block would fire up and set off the huge amount of explosives packed in the back. "Just a few minutes more," he said to himself.

Chief Inspector Seabridge positioned himself at the top of King Street where it meets Cross Street. He had a view of the van, off to his left, and when he looked straight ahead, across the road, he was surprised to see his colleague, Inspector Comerford, who was with the soldiers in Back Pool Fold.

The Inspector later explained: "I was the only one around when the bomb squad arrived, so I ended up taking them to a point from where they could see the van and operate their equipment. They parked their two vans in Cross Street at a slight angle. I was to discover shortly afterwards that this configuration was an important barrier in an explosion."

By 11.10am the cordon was as far back as it was going, held at approximately a quarter of a mile from the van with a circumference of more than one and a half miles. There was never any decision to hold it there, it was just that the circle was now so expanded that the police were stretched to the absolute limit and to go further would mean leaving gaps through which foolish folk would be able to pass. They had run out of the blue police evacuation tape and had started using yellow tape normally used for crime scene preservation.

The nearest place to the van where civilians were still congregated was, as the crow flies – or the bomb blasts – Kendals department store on Deansgate. They sheltered under its canopy, directly in front of the ten-feet-high floor-to-ceiling plate glass windows displaying smart dresses draped over mannequins. But they were well out of sight of the van, around two 90 degree corners, one right, one left. The people cramming the street perceived no danger. They could never have anticipated that the power of the explosion was going to hurtle around the bends like a laser-guided missile and put many of them in hospital.

Reports were coming in about other suspect devices within the cordon, small ones, perhaps designed, like the previous Manchester IRA bombs in 1992, to maim evacuees. On that occasion one bomb went off outside an office block in St Mary's Street at around 8am, causing damage but no casualties. A second, left in a bag by some steps leading from a shopping area off Cateaton Street, exploded as people were being evacuated down them. Astonishingly, no-one was badly hurt. Four years on and police made a decision to ignore these reports for the time being as, by this stage, any small device posed no risk to life, only to property. In the event the rumours were erroneous.

The four-strong Army group said they were preparing to disrupt the device with a controlled explosion. From Back Pool Fold Inspector Comerford acted as liaison and spoke into his radio. His words were to become the stuff of legend.

"For information," he said, "the EOD (Explosive Ordnance Disposal) are ready to start their operation. There will be two explosions, one small one and one slightly larger. Please stay out of sight of the van."

The police helicopter, call-sign India 99, which had been using its Skyshout loudspeaker system to help with the evacuation, took up a hover position more than a mile from the van, looking down on it from the north with a video camera whirring. They could see the robot by the side of the Cargo, its 16-inch long gun arm held delicately aloft, like a baton in the fingers of an orchestra's conductor. The pilot and the crew held their collective breath.

From the same vantage point an hour earlier the streets around had resembled an ant colony, people like specks, flowing along the pavements. Even minutes before there had been a scampering of individuals and pockets of people on the move. Now there was no-one. Nothing living. Just the vehicle, the robot and the bomb.

Watching his monitors in the control room, satisfied the area was clear of people, of potential casualties, Chief Superintendent Harris gave his approval for the bomb squad to begin their operation.

The first noise was a barely audible crumpling sound as the first charge tore through the vehicle's skin, exposing the bomb's detonator. Taking another few seconds to manoeuvre into position, the Army team prepared to use their secondary tactic designed to destroy the device's primer, rendering it safe without detonating its huge payload of home-made fertilizer.

A closed-circuit TV camera, normally used to monitor traffic, was watching the whole process and sending back pictures to the control room where Mr Harris was watching, scarcely daring to blink.

With a stab of horror he saw a woman appear on one of the screens on the bridge immediately above the Cargo lorry. She had somehow remained in the Arndale Centre despite the evacuation. The noise of the first explosion sent her scuttling back inside. She was extraordinarily lucky to survive.

The clock in the office clicked from 11.16 to 11.17 and four seconds later his screen went blank. A second after that the boom of the explosion shook the room and several windows in his police station blew in.

Without warning, the van had detonated and hurled debris a mile into the sky. The timer had beaten the Army by one second.

Chapter Two

A Hard Rain

"IT was so loud it was a physical thing," said Chief Inspector Seabridge who was as close to the explosion as anyone. "For a second all my senses had gone and I was confused to the point I didn't immediately realise that it was the IRA bomb that had exploded and not the Army's. It was like a sonic boom, the noise alone pressing down with real force. Although I was close, the actual blast missed me completely but I still felt the power of the noise.

"Seconds later it started to rain, like the heavy rain of a summer storm, except there were no clouds and it wasn't water. It was debris and flying glass. Momentarily I wanted to look up at the rain but my brain went into survival mode and reminded me it was masonry and I should keep my head down.

"The sound changed again, this time to a patter-patter as it all started to hit the ground. My first instinct was to get in close to buildings for shelter but then I realised that huge shards of glass were coming out of their frames so I moved away again and made instead for the middle of the street. The whole thing was over in seconds though it seemed like a lifetime, and the upshot was I ended up pretty much where I started.

"The next stage was the clump-clump-clump sound of bigger debris, including the van itself, coming back to earth. That was followed by another fine rain, this caused by the lighter stuff which had been propelled even higher.

"When I moved to look around the corner there was a huge mushroom cloud of dust and debris. As I was watching I came to realise the noises had stopped and there was a sudden air of stillness."

A view from the detonation site down Cross Street past the Royal Exchange

Inspector Comerford, protected by the overhang of an alcove, flattened himself into the recess of the alleyway as the glass and masonry fell around him. "There was an unbelievable noise and a blast of heat and compression," he said. "The next thing, all the surrounding windows fell down on me." His cap was blown off and when the air cleared there was a half-inch covering of glass on his head. His first thought was that he was going to be permanently deaf.

"Giant shards of glass came out of the building," he said. "Then the glass became smaller and smaller and when it looked like rain it was quite beautiful, it glittered. It was like being at the centre of a gorgeous, inexplicable glow. Then the lovely day was suddenly dark and cooler because the sun had been blocked out. Orange glass powder settled on my shoulders. It had only been moments but I had been transported somewhere else for those seconds. Now I was back in reality. In the control room they all thought we were dead."

Comerford's only physical injury was a cut to his ear and he was known from then on as 'Lucky Dave', but he later suffered from depression brought on by the experience and needed time off work, though he returned to full duty.

Inspector Hal Hymanson was 300 yards away from the van, ushering stragglers back, when it exploded and he was concussed by the shock wave. Nevertheless, he spent another nine hours in the immediate area as the dust continued to settle. Less than a year later he was suffering from throat cancer. There was no history of the disease in his family and the strain afflicting him was normally associated with heavy smoking and drinking of which he did neither. A report he obtained from the University of Manchester Institute of Science and Technology concluded that a post-explosion dust cloud may have contained cancer-causing chemicals when it descended on the city. Asbestos was certainly recognised as a problem at the time. Inspector Hymanson made a full recovery after treatment.

One of the soldiers from the bomb squad was injured by flying debris and others felt the pressure of the blast but none was seriously hurt.

The shock-wave travelled at a mind-boggling 2,000 metres per second through, over and around buildings in loops and curves in a manner rarely before experienced.

A pregnant woman standing at the opposite end of the Arndale Centre from the blast site was thrown fifteen feet through the air and knocked unconscious. Pcs Emma Thompson and Gary Hartley had bravely gone to check a suggestion that people were sheltering in a cellar too close to the vehicle and were caught in the open less than 200 yards from the blast. They were seen standing in the road outside the Corn Exchange with their hands over their heads while murderous debris landed all around them but mercifully – miraculously, it was said later – it missed them both.

Four firefighters who had been helping with the evacuation were at the back of Longridge House, next to M&S, which housed the Royal Insurance Company and had not been evacuated. A stunned security guard staggered out and told them there were still seventeen people inside.

He was immediately followed by a group of women, all covered in blood, who said there were more injured upstairs. The firemen ran past them, up the stairs to the second floor where they found victims huddled together in the centre of the room, some screaming and crying, others silent and rocking to and fro. The explosion had shattered every window that surrounded their open-plan office. Sections of the ceiling were hanging down, workstations had been tossed aside and slid across the floor, shards of glass were everywhere, some embedded in desks. One woman was buried under a heap of shelving and cupboards.

Two of the firemen helped these victims while two others ran up another flight of stairs to check other offices. They were met by two more women, also smothered in blood and traumatised. The men asked if there was anyone else upstairs and, through sobs, one replied: "Yes, but they're all dead".

Steeling themselves, the two firemen stepped up another flight and into another open-plan office utterly destroyed by the power of the bomb. Three people lay immobile in the wreckage, cut and battered by flying debris. But they were alive.

Pc Hartley arrived and carried one desperately wounded woman down the stairs on his back. She was the most seriously injured victim of the detonation, 42-year-old Barbara Welch, from Preston. She had been by a window looking at the van when it detonated less than 100 yards away. Her face was ripped by countless tiny shards of glass and she required 300 stitches in seven hours of surgery. Consultant surgeon Peter White likened the task of rebuilding her face to putting together a jigsaw. It was, he said, one of the most difficult challenges he has ever had to deal with. But twelve months later she had made a remarkable recovery, physically and psychologically, and was back at work.

One of the firemen who helped her was assistant divisional officer Dave Morris. Twelve years previously an IRA car bomb had killed his brother-in-law, a soldier serving in Northern Ireland. He was later to say: "I think I am a stronger person for having lived through the Manchester bomb experience. The city really pulled impressively together afterwards. Out of devastation came a lot of good."

The momentary shocked silence of the city was suddenly shattered by the sounds of people everywhere screaming in terror and pain, and the endless clamour of hundreds of activated alarm systems. Police radios chattered into life, exchanging information about damage and calling for ambulances for casualties by the hundred, but amazingly, nearly all minor.

Most of the shoppers who, seconds earlier, had been standing impatiently outside Kendals' large plate glass windows were now stampeding down Deansgate. Others were unable to move because the windows exploded outwards and were fired across the street cutting down victims. Bloodied shoppers lay motionless on the pavement, for all the world like corpses. Many traumatised witnesses left the scene certain in the knowledge that they had just watched scores of people die. Others among the injured were screaming or crying. Yet more were staring at their wounds in horrified disbelief, trying to come to terms with what had just happened.

The sudden knowledge that this was a bomb – a huge one – and not a harmless but annoying bomb *scare* like so many others triggered mass panic. The idea of there being a second bomb in the area was a rumour that spread like wildfire. Each car and van was viewed with wide-eyed suspicion. Any of them could explode at any second and create still more carnage. People just ran until they could no longer, dragging children with them, half carrying elderly relatives. All the time debris was landing and damaged windows continued to shed heavy shards of glass and each loud smash as another hit the ground sent quivers of fear through those in flight.

The plume of smoke soared into the sky, dwarfing the city's skyscrapers, and could be seen more than ten miles away. The relatives and friends of the thousands caught under its billowing canopy were aware within minutes something terrible had happened, but had no way of knowing the scale. Panic gripped communities around Manchester as they considered the unspeakable possibility that their husbands, wives, children, parents, could all be dead.

Amongst the fleeing crowds a Big Issue seller stood in the road, totally traumatised and unable to speak coherently. A woman ambled along the pavement, apparently sleep walking, such was the depth of her shock.

Both windows at either end of the late-evacuated STA Travel shop were blasted out and lethal glass shrapnel was scattered across the desks and tables.

Chief Inspector Seabridge saw a baby, covered in blood, being put in a police Land Rover. "Tomorrow was Father's Day and I suddenly thought of my own three-month-old son safe at home. I was later deeply relieved to discover that though it looked dreadful the child had suffered only minor injuries."

Comerford found a shocked teenage boy who had been separated from his mother and was terrified that she might have been killed. He looked after him and made sure he got help. The following day, when the Inspector was policing a Euro '96 football match at Old Trafford, he was astonished when the same boy stepped out of the huge crowd. "Thank you for what you did," the boy said. "My mother is safe. She got home."

Sgt Naughton had moved his section of the cordon back as far as

Chetham's School of Music near Victoria Station, a full 700 yards from the van with several large buildings in-between.

"I was starting the breathe normally again and feeling deep relief at being safe at last after being so close to the van for what seemed an eternity" he said. "I looked up and suddenly noticed how wonderfully blue the sky was that morning. Then, it was just like when you put on a pair of sunglasses. In a moment the blue turned to grey and this huge explosion shook the earth."

Out of the darkness, from very high up, a small object came into his focus, spinning extremely quickly. Its velocity was such that, though he knew it was going to hit him, he had no time to avoid it. Maybe he moved just a little, maybe that saved his life.

It was a piece or concrete, half the size of a soccer ball. It shaved the top of his shoulder and ripped off his epaulet bearing his sergeant's chevrons. The formidable force created by its momentum sent a shock wave down his arm and across his chest producing an instant bruise, damaging tendons and joints. The blow from the supersonic 'missile' cut his skin but cauterised the wound at the same time.

Then the shock wave knocked him off his feet and, as he lay on the ground, more small objects cascaded from the sky, falling on to his legs, cutting them. Despite his injuries and the onset of shock, because he was convinced a second bomb was likely – as in the previous IRA attack on Manchester – he commandeered a Metrolink tram from Victoria Station to take 50 walking wounded to North Manchester General Hospital.

"As we stepped outside Crumpsall station we could see people mowing their lawns and there was an ice cream van which seemed out of place after what we been through a couple of stops down the line," he said. "Here was normal life and then all these people staggered out of the station covered in blood."

A little earlier the hospital had already been busy with Casualty struggling to cope with the remnants of the weekend wounded from the boozy Friday night before in the pubs and clubs. Much of the expertise on duty was also dealing with two very seriously injured patients, one the victim of a nasty road crash and the other a building worker whose spine had been crushed by a toppled pile of bricks. All this was causing delays in A&E and one waiting patient decided he would wait no more and demanded immediate treatment. He became so aggressive that a worried receptionist dialled 999.

"Sorry," said the police operator. "We're a bit pushed." The time was 11.15am. Two minutes later they heard the explosion four miles away and the windows in the hospital shook. It was only a few minutes more before a policeman ran through the entrance doors cradling a child whose leg had been sliced open by flying glass. More casualties rolled up in cars, ambulances and buses before the train disembarked. A total of 79 people were treated there and a further 80 at Manchester Royal infirmary. Others were dealt with on the street by ambulance crews and doctors and nurses who were already in the city centre.

The blast ran north to south for a full mile from the beginning of Bury New Road to the Midland Hotel. Westwards, it reached the Portland Thistle Hotel and to the East crossed the River Irwell. The fact that no-one died still bemuses those who were there to witness such power unleashed.

Many office and shop staff had been ushered into basements for their safety and were stuck down there for several hours while checks were made that there were no other bombs. Throughout the lunchtime period and early afternoon there were huge queues at phone boxes with people desperately wanting to reassure their families they were safe, this at a time before most of the population possessed a mobile.

The 50 Saturday staff at the Co-operative Bank in Balloon Street, all working on the upper floors, had been told to stay indoors but away from windows, as that was considered the safest thing to do with the lorry a good 250 yards away. When it exploded with that enormous bang part of the vehicle, including a heavy bolt, landed in the roof garden on the second floor. The building shook and ceiling tiles fell on to staff inside, but all but two of the windows were covered with protective film following the previous

Manchester bombs and survived intact. The unclad windows shattered but not in rooms where people were gathered and no-one was injured.

Dust filled the offices and the shocked workers had to stay inside for another 90 minutes before they were advised it was safe to evacuate.

At that point the head office of a major clearing bank with 1.5 million customers and assets of £2.3 billion was empty and would remain so for another four days until the cordon was pulled back. However, all the computer operations were run from other sites in Skelmersdale, Salford and Stockport, so key workers were directed to those locations and emergency procedures, put in place after the last IRA attack on Manchester, proved their worth with the bank remaining operational, though its head office was not fully open until the following Monday, nine days after the bomb

Public transport came to a standstill, car parks were inaccessible and many cars had been destroyed or damaged beyond the capability of being driven. Workers who had evacuated, leaving their belongings behind, found themselves without keys, wallets and handbags. Stunned, people walked out of the city and picked up transport where they could. The centre, so busy a short time before, cleared of life. It was like the aftermath of a bombing raid half a century previously, silent except for the sound of sirens. Not air raid warnings this time but hundreds of burglar alarms blasting away, screaming their fury. They would continue for days.

Two men saw the positive side and were arrested while looting shops after they sneaked under the tape. The tills were packed with money but surprisingly little was stolen.

That evening Chief Inspector Seabridge walked though the devastated area. "It was dusk and the sound of alarm sirens was everywhere," he recalled. "Bits of masonry were still dropping off buildings and when I turned a corner and saw a mannequin hanging out of a shop window like a dead body I couldn't help but jump. By that time, seven hours or so after the explosion, we knew that more than 200 people had been injured, but few seriously, and we were fairly sure that despite the devastation no-one had been killed. One of the beggars who usually sat outside Marks and

Spencer's with his blanket was missing, but it turned out he had gone for his fix and turned up later in Stockport. We were not looking for bodies under the rubble because we were confident we had got everyone out of the immediate area before the explosion.

"It was then that our thoughts turned towards the bricks and mortar of the city, to the awesome damage that had been done. That night I didn't get much sleep though I was very tired, as it all ran though my mind again and again. When Sunday came it was a relief to begin to return to normality, to see what had to be done and begin the work."

Chief Superintendent Harris, who spent the next week living in his police station's flat, has considered the potential for utter disaster many times. "On the day we were able, just, to evacuate sufficiently and prevented what would have been many deaths and serious injuries but, if this event had happened on a weekday, the number of people in the immediate area would have been double the 80,000 we managed to move. Succeeding in an evacuation of that size within the time-scale would have been much more difficult.

"After the event the IRA sent a message purporting to be an apology for the bombing. They claimed they had not intended for it to go off because they expected the Army bomb squad would diffuse it and suggesting they had given us plenty of time to move people away. It absolutely infuriated me. They wanted an explosion and had scant regard for human life. It was an act of pure evil. My first thought was; how dare they? How dare they say they regret the injuries to civilians when they planted and primed the biggest bomb ever detonated on the mainland in the middle of a busy shopping area, a place full of mothers and children the day before Fathers' Day? How dare they claim to regret injuring civilians when so many of the people hurt were well behind safety zones but cut to ribbons nevertheless because the blast was so huge?"

Eileen Comerford, the Inspector's wife, was working at a church café in Stockport, eight miles away, when she heard the distant bang. If she had gone upstairs she would have been able to see the cloud billowing over the city. Instead she continued to work until a traumatised passer-by, his ear glued to his radio, told everyone in the shop manically, "Manchester has been devastated. The city has gone. It was on the radio."

She went white. She knew there was no point in calling Bootle Street police station, she'd never get through and anyway, everyone sufficiently able would be out doing what they could, so she went home and waited anxiously by the phone. Eventually, after what seemed an age, it rang and she snatched it up and heard her husband's voice.

"I'm alive," he told her. "We all are."

Assistant Chief Constable Ian Seabridge

Chapter Three

Fallout

IN the immediate aftermath of the blast, the fact that the massive device had not claimed a single fatality was dubbed "The Miracle of Manchester". It served as an optimistic headline, as did the defiant rhetoric from council leader Richard Leese, who declared: "Manchester will be back on its feet to fight another day." The harsh reality was, however, that a ton and a half of high explosive, detonated on the surface in a confined area enclosed by tall buildings, has a devastating impact and when the dust had settled, the extent of the destruction in the heart of Manchester's shopping centre stunned those first on the scene.

Marks and Spencer's 'wavy' canopy

Close to the epicentre of the blast, the damage was colossal. The quirky landmark "wavy" canopy of Marks & Spencer's store in Corporation Street hung from the shattered façade at a crazy drunken angle and the bridge spanning the street between M&S and the Arndale shopping centre at first floor level had been all but brought down. A 60-metre section of the frontage of the Arndale itself had been torn away by the force of the explosion, exposing the centre's concrete skeleton, and the marbled malls inside were strewn with debris. Nearby, the seven-storey Longridge House, where Mrs Welch was injured, was damaged beyond repair.

Why us? That was the question on everyone's lips. Ten years on, the only answer is speculative. According to Professor Richard English of Queen's University, Belfast, the order for such large scale attacks as the Manchester bomb could have only come directly from the top level of the IRA, the Army Council. Professor English, whose history of the IRA, *Armed Struggle* is regarded as the definitive account of the Irish republican terror organisation, told BBC television's *Inside Out* documentary programme: "A bombing like this would not have happened without their say so."

The base of Longridge House

It happened between ceasefires; the IRA had a ceasefire between 1994 and 1996 which was ended by the bomb in London's docklands on 10th February, 1996, which killed two people. Their so-called justification for that, for the subsequent Manchester attack and others, was that the British government was refusing to engage with their political wing, Sinn Fein, and seek a political solution. Instead, the IRA claimed, the British were still seeking IRA defeat.

"With the Manchester bomb, the IRA was really saying: 'Look what we can do'," explained Professor English. "This was their biggest-ever bomb so it was a way of saying, not so much: 'We're back at war,' but: 'If we have another ceasefire you have to deal with us.' The choice of the city itself was party based on long-standing IRA thinking that bombs in England had always got far more attention than bombs in Northern Ireland."

The choice of Manchester specifically, was probably also partly influenced by the fact that people and media organisations from all over Europe had gathered in the city for Euro '96. What Margaret Thatcher called "the oxygen of publicity" on which terror groups thrive, was guaranteed.

John Stalker, the former Deputy Chief Constable of Greater Manchester, had been in the city on the day of the explosion with his young granddaughter when he heard the unmistakeable "crump" of the detonation and beat a hasty retreat. Stalker's high-flying police career had been, he believes, deliberately destroyed by a conspiracy when it became clear his controversial investigation into the Northern Ireland security services' alleged "shoot to kill" policy appeared on the brink of causing extreme political discomfort at Stormont and in Westminster. His take on the bomb that shattered the centre of his home town was typically robust.

"The IRA was intending to create sheer terror in exactly the same way as carpet bombing during the war," he explained. "It was a means of beating people into submission. The sheer size of the Manchester bomb clearly was not intended as a warning; this was intended to change attitudes."

In the immediate aftermath there was bewilderment – and anger too - that Manchester had been singled out and dealt such a savage blow. Ken

Eastham, then Labour MP for the north Manchester Parliamentary seat of Blackley, summed up the mood in a House of Commons speech. "We were shocked by the hatred poured on to the city," he declared. "We have always prided ourselves on good relationships with the north and south of Ireland; we have exchanges with them and there are plenty of Irish people living in the city. We were shocked by what happened to us; it was a dastardly, cold-blooded act by evil people.

"It happened on a Saturday morning in a busy part of central Manchester which was peopled mostly by women and children doing their shopping. Do not let us kid ourselves and say that it was a rebellion against the system only intended to damage property. The bomb was placed right in the centre of the population – about 80,000 people were going about their business and enjoying themselves. They were shattered by that dirty, evil and unforgivable act. What I saw in the aftermath, women and children pouring with blood and having to be evacuated, is engraved on my heart."

The late Lord Dean of Beswick - as Joe Dean he had been housing chairman and leader of Manchester city council before becoming a Leeds MP – described his own shock at the destruction wrought on his home city by the bombers. A Mancunian through and through who had worked in the same Metro-Vicks engineering factory as Fred Lee, Minister of Power in Harold Wilson's government in the 1960s, and Hugh Scanlon, president of the Amalgamated Engineering Union, told the House of Lords: "In my youth I was on fire-watching duty in Deansgate, Manchester, but I never saw surface damage like that inflicted by this bomb. Bombs from aircraft penetrate, explode and leave a crater, but this was almost total surface damage, scything everything in front of it. The prompt action of the police and fire brigade was magnificent, shifting 80,000 people in a short time out of an area half a mile in diameter. My daughter was working 50 yards the other side of the wall from the site of the bomb."

Lord Dean pleaded in the Lords debate for special help for small businesses whose owners were not being allowed back into their premises because of the danger of collapse and didn't even know if they had any stock left.

In all, the bomb had left more than half a million square feet of retail shops and 600,000 square feet of office space completely wrecked or badly damaged, displacing 670 businesses, large and small.

A significant number were in the Arndale Centre, which occupied 26 acres between Market Street, Shudehill, Corporation Street and High Street. It had been constructed between 1972 and 1979 at a cost of £100m, replacing a warren of Victorian back streets. The monolithic building straddling Cannon Street bus station comprised more than 200 shops and stores, several residential flats and an office tower – then the third tallest in the city. When completed it was the biggest city centre indoor shopping complex in Europe, visited by 750,000 people each week.

The complex may have been unloved for its exterior, but it was an undoubted success in commercial terms, having moved into the nation's top ten shopping venues at number seven when the bombers struck. The blast took out 240 firms large and small and when the extent of the destruction was first revealed there were pessimistic claims that a third of the Arndale might have to be demolished. Actually, it grew much bigger in following years, but when salvage teams first entered the debris-strewn malls wearing masks because non-refrigerated fruit, meat and fish from the market had gone rotten and was giving off an all-pervading putrid stench, much of the complex appeared beyond rescue.

Richard Christmas, then managing director of P&O Shopping Centres, said: "The devastation was appalling, dreadful, and shocking. There was glass and debris all over the place and the alarms were ringing out a cacophony of noise. Fashion store dummies had fallen out of shattered shop windows and littered the floor like bodies. It was eerie – just like Beruit." He had been on a day off when the bomb exploded and returned to find his office walls "like dartboards" where they had been peppered by flying shrapnel.

Just across the road, Marks and Spencer's fourth biggest UK store was in ruins. Senior company managers were not given access to the wrecked building until Tuesday, June 18th. At 11.30am, almost exactly three days after the bomb exploded, specialist teams who had been assembled throughout the weekend went in to assess the extent of the damage. Their efforts, however, were soon restricted when, within a few hours, health and safety experts from the local authority served a "Condemned Site" notice on the building, barring the way to the extensive office tower block which served as a regional administrative centre for five other stores in the North West and where the staff's personal belongings and records remained.

The circumstances dictated, however, that it was not a place to linger. Like the Arndale, the putrid smell from the food store, where perishable stocks had by then been without refrigeration for 72 hours, was permeating the entire building. The process of removing it eventually took seven days and nights of intense manual effort, with conditions worsening all the time before all of it was cleared. It a was almost a week after the explosion before all the money could be removed from the sales floor tills and the cash room, and not until Saturday June 22nd that specialist teams started the removal of staff possessions – and even then, because of a possible contamination risk from asbestos, that task had to be carried out under controlled conditions.

When the wreckage was totted up, retailers that suffered major structural damage in the blast included Marks & Spencer (60,000 square feet), Argos (40,000 square feet), Top Man (15,000 square feet), Boots and WH Smith (both 10,000 square feet), the clothing store USC (5,000 square feet) and Dorothy Perkins (2,000 square feet). Partial structural damage was sustained by British Home Stores (40,000 square feet), Littlewoods (40,000 square feet) and the Ramada Hotel on Deansgate (40,000 square feet).

Though the destruction of Marks and Spencer's and the west frontage of the Arndale Centre – both relatively modern buildings - were the most obvious effects of the blast, the power of the explosion also inflicted grave damage on a number of the city's historic landmarks.

One of those closest to the bomb – just 50 yards away - was the Royal Exchange, its theatre within, rightly regarded as one of the jewels in the North West's arts crown. The vast building was the third Royal Exchange on the site, completed in 1874. Ten times the size of the original of 1729, it reflected the commercial power and status of 19th Century Manchester. Its massive trading floor, measuring 206 feet by 96 feet beneath a huge dome soaring 125 feet above was, at the time, easily the largest commercial room in the world. By 1913 the Royal Exchange had more than 10,000 members, requiring a further extension which was opened by King George V and Queen Mary in 1921.

After suffering bomb damage in World War II, the building was reopened by Princess Margaret in 1953 but with King Cotton in steep decline, it never resumed its previous level of trading. On New Year's Eve 1968 the great hall was closed and remained so until September 1976 when it was reborn as the Royal Exchange Theatre and opened by Sir Lawrence Olivier. The revolutionary 800-seat theatre in the round – a steel structure sitting in the middle of the former trading floor – staged major productions and brought a galaxy of stars such as Tom Courtney, Albert Finney, John Thaw, Vanessa Redgrave and Julie Walters to Manchester.

The cultural gem took a colossal blow and there were real fears that the structure of the building had been irreparably weakened. Michael Williams, building manager in charge of the reconstruction work, explained: "Bomb blasts come in two waves; you have the pressure wave which compresses everything and then you have the vacuum that comes after it, and that did an enormous amount of damage to the structure of the building. Strangely enough, it didn't look that bad, but it took a year to investigate what had actually happened before we could even start."

The glass dome had collapsed and every pane of glass in the building and every inch of the interior had to be re-plastered and repainted. The Royal Exchange could be saved, but the bill would come to £31 million.

The Royal Exchange's ground floor, basement and part of the first floor had been an upscale specialist shopping centre comprising more than 70 traders, including jewellers, perfumeries, fashion boutiques, coffee and confectionery businesses and an antiques market supported by several cafes and bistros. The area was badly damaged and the small-to-medium business concerns were among those most at risk during what was to be a two-year shut-down. Likewise, scores of small businesses that plied their trade at Manchester's Corn Exchange, 500 yards from ground zero in the other direction, were bombed out.

The Corn Exchange, a huge, triangular building was opened in Hanging Ditch, close to the Cathedral in 1905, replacing a building dating from 1835 on the same site. It had been an important regional centre for the trading of agricultural produce and one of few in this area of the city to survive the Manchester "Blitz" of December 1940. Behind its imposing Grade II listed Edwardian façade, the Corn Exchange was rather less grand in its latter years, becoming shabby and run down, with its cavernous galleried interior occupied by an enduringly popular indoor flea market specialising in "New Age" artefacts and services. The bomb ended that role in an instant; the central glass dome above the enormous trading floor was lifted upwards by the blast and completely destroyed when it crashed down again. All 800 roof panels were also blown away.

Curiously, a group of eccentric new age "psychogeographers" had publicly announced themselves in Manchester on February 10th 1996 by performing their first "Action" – the levitation of the Corn Exchange – to commemorate the 400th anniversary of the arrival in the city of Dr John Dee, warden of the Collegiate Church which was later to become Manchester Cathedral. Dee was a 16th Century alchemist, historian and cartographer in the court of Queen Elizabeth I and arguably the inspiration for Prospero in Shakespeare's The Tempest. His house was rumoured to have stood on the site occupied by the Corn Exchange and he would approved of the "alternative" Saturday market. Members of the Manchester Area Psychogeographic, as the group called itself, circumnavigated the site anti-clockwise and claimed, in all seriousness, that they had "watched the building move". Moreover they alleged that staff in a ground floor fish and chip shop concurred. The tremor felt four months later, courtesy of the IRA bombers, however, measured considerably higher on the Richter scale.

Manchester Cathedral was damaged too and not for the first time in its long history. Built over a period of 600 years from 1215, it was chartered as the Collegiate Church of St Mary, St Denys and St George by the Lancastrian

King Henry V in 1421. Legend has it that St Denys, Patron Saint of France, is included because the King, the victor at Agincourt, wanted his claim to the French throne recognised. Its treasures were plundered during the reign of Edward VI in 1550 and again during the English Civil War in 1649. When the Manchester diocese was created in 1847, the Collegiate Church was named the city's Cathedral and extensive rebuilding took place throughout the 19th Century. In December 1940, during World War II, it suffered a direct hit from a German bomb which landed in the Regimental Chapel for the Manchester Regiment and blew out the windows; something of a blessing, for, despite the extensive damage, the safety valve effect enabled the structure and the ornate woodwork of the interior to escape complete destruction. Restoration work, however took 20 years.

The Cathedral was damaged again on 3rd December 1992 when the second of two relatively small IRA bombs detonated in nearby Cateaton Street. The blast smashed the clock in the Cathedral tower and shattered Victorian stained glass windows, showering hundreds of people who had sought refuge there from a bomb that had exploded 85 minutes earlier a quarter of a mile away in St Mary's Street.

In 1996 it was the south side of the cathedral that took the brunt of the blast. The force lifted the roof, which, astonishingly, fell back into place undamaged. But damage to the windows ran to almost £200,000 as most of those facing south were blown out. They were mostly plain Victorian panes but there was also an ornate red-stained glass design in the Regimental Chapel, a commemoration, ironically, of the 1940 Manchester blitz. The office where the then Dean of Manchester, the Very Reverend Ken Riley, had been sitting half an hour before, was strewn with debris and lethal shards of glass. Had he stayed, he later observed, he could have been the only fatality of the bomb.

The then Bishop of Manchester, the Right Reverend Christopher Mayfield, who was at a meeting with other Church leaders when the bomb detonated, said: "The IRA need to hear that they are living in a fantasy world. They need to renounce their weapons, renounce terrorism and get down to listening and talking peace with others as concerned about Ireland as they are."

Despite the damage, the Cathedral was open for an ecumenical service for the whole community the following Saturday and 2,000 people attended. Shopkeepers, members of the emergency services, civic and religious leaders all joined together for what was described as a service of reconciliation. Among the congregation were many of the city's walking wounded, still shocked by the huge explosion.

Later, like the wider city centre, the Cathedral was to reap the benefits of the rebuilding programme which made it the centre of Manchester's newly designated Millennium Quarter complete with, for the first time, its own Visitor Centre.

Manchester's second most important church was also damaged. Consecrated by the Bishop of Chester in July, 1712, the church was dedicated to St. Ann, the Virgin Mary's Mother, as a compliment both to its founder and to the reigning Queen; indeed it nursed a lengthy affinity with the royal Stuart cause. Among the church's early congregants was John Byrom, author of Christians Awake, who, like many Mancunians of the time harboured Jacobite sympathies during the rebellions of 1715 and 1745 - direct results of that talismanic event in Irish history, William of Orange's victory over James II at the Battle of the Boyne - though by the time of the second insurrection Manchester merchants had begun to discover that political faction interfered with trade, and were ready to pay only nostalgic lip-service to the Stuart cause.

Prince Charles Edward – Bonny Prince Charlie - advanced in November 1745, taking Lancaster, Preston and Wigan on his way to Manchester which he entered on November 28th. The Rector of St. Ann's, the Reverend Joseph Hoole, had died the day before and, as he and his curate had preached against rebellion from St. Ann's pulpit, his widow deemed it prudent to bury him with all speed in case the Pretender's soldiers disturbed the funeral. Despite her precautions, some of the Highland officers entered the Square at the same time as the funeral procession but, far from causing a disturbance, they removed their bonnets and joined in the service. The Bonny Prince's triumphs were not to endure for long: after retreat from Derby his forces suffered a final defeat at Culloden Moor and the 1745 rebellion was over.

The IRA left a more serious mark on the church. A National Lottery-funded £240,000 refurbishment of St Ann's was nearing completion when their bomb blasted out the upper level gallery windows and their frames, covered the nave and gallery with shards of glass and left three major stained glass windows holed and cracked. The bill amounted to another £130,000. The Verger, Charles Longley, and Roger the flower seller, a familiar figure in St Ann's Square, were uninjured having retreated to the tower room when the warning was sounded. They calculated that they would be safe behind three-feet-thick stone walls and besides, one of the refugees was Church of England and the other a Roman Catholic. God, they decided, would be on the side of at least one of them.

The blast that tore through Marks & Spencer's store came out of the other side to hit one of Manchester's oldest buildings full on, but remarkably, the Old Shambles, a venerable relic from Mediaeval times, remained standing and, compared with the devastation wrought upon the store just a few yards away, relatively unscathed. The half-timbered Old Wellington Inn, dating from 1552 and Sinclair's Oyster Bar, built 168 years later, were and remain remarkable survivors down the centuries. The Victorians, who showed scant regard for the built heritage of their predecessors, tore down virtually all of Manchester's Mediaeval structures save for the Cathedral and Chetham's School, and by the end of the 19th Century the Old Shambles was completely surrounded by their works. But much of the area was in turn flattened by the Luftwaffe and until the early 1970s the Old Shambles stood by the side of flower gardens that marked the triangular site of Victoria Buildings, destroyed by German bombs in 1940.

Originally, the Old Wellington Inn was part residence and part draper's shop. It was not until 1830 that the premises were licensed, when it was known first as The Vintners' Arms and later, The Kenyon Vaults. In 1865, the ground floor became the Wellington Inn, while the upper two floors served as a mathematical and optical instrument maker's workshop. By 1897, the upper floors were known as "Ye Old Fyshing Tackle Shoppe".

An even bigger threat than those posed by the Victorians or overhead Heinkel 111s arrived in the early 1970s when the pubs were considered to be in the way of plans for Market Place, part of the massive redevelopment scheme that saw the building of the Arndale Centre and Marks & Spencer. Instead of demolishing them, however, developers raised the pubs fifteen feet above their original level to accommodate service roads and parking space below. The result was hardly a triumph; Market Place became the grimmest aspect of an unlovely scheme and the Mediaeval remnants, lost amid the brutal concrete precinct, looked like refugees from a theme park.

Now it was the turn of the IRA, but unlike their inappropriate surroundings, the Old Shambles was to survive once more; though not in the same place.

The Arndale Centre suffered massive damage

Chapter Four

Shock

ON the morning that the city centre was blown apart, councillor Richard Leese was in the town hall in the middle of a Labour Party meeting called to analyse the results of the local elections that had taken place six weeks before. Shortly after polling had confirmed Labour's perennial grip on the council, Leese had succeeded Graham Stringer as its leader; the latter having secured the nomination as Labour's Parliamentary candidate for the safe seat of Blackley, north Manchester, in the General Election anticipated the following year.

Stringer, who had been council leader since 1984, had wanted to remain so for some months more; Leese had pressed for an immediate handover of the reins following the 1996 elections and had his way. As Alfred Waterhouse's landmark neo-gothic town hall was shaken to its foundations by the massive bomb 500 yards away at the far end of Cross Street, he might well have wished he'd agreed to Stringer remaining in office. There had been no warning for the occupants of the town hall's splendidly-appointed banqueting room that morning. "The police weren't to know we were in there," said Leese. "It was a private party meeting." Ironically, the leadership change had been the subject of debate at the meeting minutes before the explosion. Mary Murphy, a Labour councillor, had asked: "What can we do to raise the new leader's profile?" The IRA provided the answer and with it, a colossal baptism of fire.

Leese looked down from the first floor window of the stateroom into Albert Square below. It was filled with people who had been ushered there out of the immediate danger area surrounding the explosive-crammed Ford

Cargo in Corporation Street.

"My first reaction was to get everyone out of the city centre completely," he said. "My second – like most people that day – was to make sure my family and friends were okay. Third was to set about checking what the hell the council's role was supposed to be in circumstances like these. It didn't seem as if there was any set script, and in any case, this was the biggest ever peacetime explosion in the UK. You can imagine it was very confused."

Leese went down to the town hall's emergency room in the basement, in reality nothing more sophisticated than a spartan committee room with direct phone links to the police and other emergency services, to satisfy himself that whatever was in the council's contingency planning procedures was actually being carried out. In fact the entire city was pretty much paralysed with a huge area cordoned off and fears that more devices had been planted at other locations as they had been previously. It was a genuine concern as, in the previous IRA bomb attack on Manchester, four years earlier, people fleeing from the first blast were injured by the second explosion. The imposition of such a wide exclusion zone meant that instant assessments of the extent of the devastation were impossible to calculate.

In the immediate aftermath, council highways personnel closed off the streets and social services staff were called in to provide counselling for the many who needed it. Leese and deputy leader Martin Pagel remained in the town hall and began fielding media inquiries from round the world. "That's something the politicians can do while leaving people with real work to do to get on with the job," quipped Leese. "There were lots of foreign journalists in town because of Euro '96 and almost as if by magic, as the city centre emptied, Albert Square slowly filled up with camera crews. I can remember going outside in the middle of the afternoon – it was a really hot, sunny day – and standing on the corner of the square. I could see down John Dalton Street one way and all the way up Princess Street and Cross Street in other directions. Apart from the gaggle of journalists in the square behind me there was nothing, absolutely nothing, moving. It was like going out into the street in an Italian town in the middle of an afternoon when everything shuts up and everybody has a four-hour break, except of course for the sound of just about every alarm in the city centre going off and music still playing in some of the abandoned shops. It was a totally surreal atmosphere."

Realising there was little that he could immediately do, Leese watched the Euro '96 match between England and Scotland on a television in the town hall. It seemed odd that life was continuing normally elsewhere as mayhem ruled in devastated Manchester. Then he went home. Later, after reports of several threats to the Irish community, Leese and Pagel went out to the Irish World Heritage Centre in Cheetham Hill and had a pint of Guinness. "We were demonstrating a serious point, that it wasn't Manchester's Irish community that were responsible for the bombing, but terrorists, and local Irish people were just as much victims of the IRA as any other Mancunian," he explained.

As it turned out, any fears of a possible backlash against the Irish community were largely ill-founded. Apart from one or two sporadic incidents of abuse, the people of Manchester were well able to make the distinction between their neighbours and Provisional IRA terrorists. The most serious incident happened in the centre of Middleton, an old mill town six miles north of the city centre. At 7.20pm on the day the bomb exploded, a gang of about ten men burst into Delaney's, a Irish themed pub in the

Martin Pagel

town's Market Place shouting: "No Surrender" and rampaged through the bar smashing furniture and leaving all but one window shattered.

For more than 150 years, the history of the city had been closely entwined with its Irish diaspora, the largest by far of successive waves of immigrants to have made the city their home. From the arrival of the Flemish weavers – victims of religious persecution in the Low Countries - at the invitation of King Edward III in the 14th Century, to 21st Century settlers from Somalia and eastern Europe, Manchester has thrived on its diversity.

The Jewish community, the biggest outside London, grew from early immigration in the 1740s, mainly from Poland. Benjamin Marks, founder of Marks & Spencer, was born and opened his first store in the city. Dr Chaim Weizmann, first president of the State of Israel, worked in the Chemistry department of the University of Manchester in 1904 and, through his friendship with C. P. Scott, legendary editor of the Manchester Guardian, was influential in Zionist lobbying of the British government which culminated in the Balfour Declaration of 1917, promising the establishment of a Jewish national homeland in Palestine. Large Caribbean, Pakistani and Bangladeshi communities have also been absorbed with relatively little friction; indeed the city enthusiastically celebrates Moss Side's colourful carnival and promotes Rusholme's enduringly popular "Curry Mile" as an important visitor attraction.

The Irish connection, though, is endemic. As early as 1841, when Manchester was growing at a phenomenal rate as the world's first industrial city, one in ten of the population was Irish and many lived in "Little Ireland", a poverty-stricken slum in the Ancoats area which Karl Marx's collaborator, Friedrich Engels, briefly a resident, described in 1845 as the "most disgusting spot of all". The area became so overcrowded during the potato famine that emigrants from Ireland, chiefly the rural west, could not be accommodated and spilled into other cities, Liverpool and Birmingham in particular.

One contemporary report suggested that 18,000 Irish inhabitants in Manchester were living in cellars, in some cases eight to a bed – if indeed they had access to a bed at all. Yet such squalor was regarded as preferable to life across the water. Even amid these privations, however, the Irish in Manchester made their mark. Fergus O'Connor, James Bronterre O'Brien and Mary Burns were leading figures in the Chartist movement, whose descendant, the Trades Union Congress, was founded in Manchester's Mechanics' Institute in 1868.

Unsurprisingly, Irish politics followed the immigrants to Manchester. On September 11th 1867, police arrested two men for acting suspiciously in a doorway. They turned out to be Fenians Colonel Thomas Kelly and Captain Timothy Deasy, two of the leading members of the Irish Republican Brotherhood. A week later when the pair – by this time recognised by the authorities as high-profile captives – were being taken from the courthouse to the county jail in Hyde Road, Ardwick, the police van was ambushed beneath a railway arch by thirty armed men. Unable to smash their way into the armoured van with axes and sledgehammers, they demanded the officer inside open the doors. Police Sergeant Brett had the misfortune to put his eye to the keyhole just as one of the attackers fired through it from the other side. Kelly and Deasy escaped and were never recaptured, though the police later arrested 29 men, including, they claimed, those who fired revolvers.

Five, William O'Mera Allen, Michael Larkin, William O'Brien, Thomas Maguire and Edward Stone, were found guilty of murder and sentenced to death. Maguire was later pardoned and discharged, Stone's sentence was commuted to life imprisonment on the eve of his intended execution, but Allen, Larkin and O'Brien were hanged in public six weeks after Sergeant Brett's murder. Annual marches to the graves of the "Manchester Martyrs" memorial in St Joseph's Roman Catholic Cemetery in Moston – their bodies had been buried in quicklime - became ritual set-piece confrontations between Irish republicans and opposing local Orangemen and sundry right wing activists at the height of the Ulster Troubles.

Most people just shrugged at the ritual lip service paid to one century-old incident in Ireland's tortured history, but the war in Northern Ireland was horrifically delivered to Manchester's doorstep in February 1974 when a bomb was secreted into the luggage hold of a coach chartered to take on-leave soldiers and their families from the city to their Army base at Catterick in North Yorkshire. The device detonated at the rear of the bus just after midnight, killing twelve of the 50 people on board, including two young children, and scattering bodies for 250 yards along the M62 motorway near Hartshead Services, south of Leeds.

The conviction of Stockport-born Judith Ward at Wakefield Crown Court the following November left major question marks. Despite her confession – and her bizarre romantic claim that she had married Provisional IRA gunman Michael McVerry, who was shot dead during a raid on a police station at Keady, South Armagh – it was accepted she could not have planted the bomb herself, merely "minded" the explosives. Sixteen years later her conviction was overturned by the Court of Appeal following the discrediting of forensic evidence. Families of the victims of that terrible night remain denied of any closure to their grief.

After that, Manchester was mercifully spared the worst consequences of the IRA's mainland terror campaign. Small incendiary devices caused minor fires in several department stores in April 1991 during a nationwide spate of similar incidents and the following year saw the blasts in St Mary's Street and Cateaton Street which inflicted 65 slight injuries and caused relatively little damage.

Thus in 1996 the question, "Why us?" was voiced as loudly by the Mancunian Irish community as any other in the city. Only three months earlier, during the week leading up to St Patrick's Day, Manchester had staged the first of its ongoing Irish Festivals, launched in person on March 10th by the Irish Republic's President, Mary Robinson, at Manchester town hall, where the Guinness flowed in splendid staterooms which had been turned into public bars for the occasion. Robinson, who became the United Nations' Commissioner for Human Rights following her seven-year presidency of Eire, had received an honorary Law degree at the University of Manchester. The festival, the biggest Irish parade anywhere in the UK, was organised by the Irish World Heritage Centre, which, complete with its foyer floored with Connemara marble, had been opened in 1984 by the republic's then Foreign Minister, Peter Barry. Despite everything, the festival has continued to flourish and played host to the likes of the Corrs, Westlife and Van Morrison.

Irish and English – and plenty of Scots too – shared their modern heroes, not least on the terraces of Manchester United's Old Trafford football stadium. The club is by far the most popular sporting organisation in the island of Ireland, north and south of the border, uniting fans of all creeds. One Irish banner unveiled at the 1999 European Champion's League final in Barcelona was emblazoned with the legend: "MUFC – the only religion."

Some speculate that the affinity dates from the Munich air crash tragedy of 1958, among whose victims was the gifted Irish player Liam Whelan, his life cut short at the age of 22, but it goes deeper than that. Among Irish favourites from north and south of the border to have pulled on United's red jersey have been George Best, Roy Keane, Shay Brennan, Tony Dunne, Harry Gregg, Sammy McIlroy, Norman Whiteside, Frank Stapleton, Denis Irwin and John O'Shea. Diehard Irish supporters even claim Sir Matt Busby as one of their own, born just outside Glasgow, but into an Irish family. And the courageous journalist Veronica Guerin was buried with Eric Cantona's shirt draped over her coffin.

Pat Karney, an influential figure in Manchester city council's ruling Labour group, had been born in Dublin and arrived in Manchester at the age of nine with his parents, settling in the working class north Manchester district of Harpurhey. He was a close associate of twelve-year city council leader Graham Stringer since he was secretary and Stringer chairman of the Manchester Central Constituency Labour Party. From childhood Karney had been well aware of the latent prejudice some felt against Irish immigrants and claims to have dropped his Dublin accent "within 24 hours" of going to school in Manchester.

"They all took the mickey out of it," he said. "Including the teachers." Like most Irish Mancunians, as Karney describes himself, the Karneys had sought to distance themselves from republican politics and the IRA's campaign of violence, never seeing it as the way forward; though that didn't stop a lot of abuse coming their way in the wake of the Birmingham bombings. Karney played the pivotal role in establishing Manchester's Irish Festival of which he was chairman. In the immediate aftermath of the 1996 bomb, the decision had to be made whether to stage a second festival amid calls that it should be cancelled.

"Why should we cancel anything?" Karney countered. "We hadn't done anything wrong. Right from the start we decided that we would not let the terrorists set the agenda for anything in Manchester. We would show them where the good Irish people of Manchester stood on violence. That was the message that the Irish in Manchester sent to the IRA: 'We are a community here. We are not being bullied by your cowardly bombs'."

Warned to evacuate by loudspeaker broadcasts from the hovering police helicopter, Karney fled from his home in the city centre's Northern Quarter and reached the police cordon around the nearby Arndale Centre only to be redirected towards Piccadilly Gardens. As he ran he heard the bomb detonate. "It was an unforgettable memory for anyone in Manchester that day," he said. Then, with hundreds of other evacuees, he heard the order from the helicopter to evacuate the centre completely. "People were panicked, wailing and crying," he said. "I remember being terrified that

Pat Karney

every car in Oldham Street could be another bomb waiting to go off."

Despite Karney's personal terror, however, he was the prime mover in encouraging Mancunians back into their wounded city centre at the earliest opportunity. Just seven days after the blast, Karney organised a family fun day in Albert Square, painting a large "I love Manchester" heart on his face. "I was criticised for it within the council Labour group at the time," he recalled. "Some said it was wrong to bring children into town so close to where the bomb had exploded and so soon afterwards. Others said nobody would come. But I wanted to try to create a carnival atmosphere to show that Manchester was up and running despite the blow it had suffered and that we weren't destroyed. Jobs were important, so we needed to show Manchester was fighting back and some normality had returned to the city, even at that early stage. In the event the square was packed with people wanting to make the same point."

The bomb propelled Karney, up to then best known for his waspish political tongue, into centre stage as chairman of the council's city centre sub-committee. It had been set up to play a co-ordinating function between policymakers and various town hall departments, but suddenly the committee became pivotal and Karney relished his heightened public profile. "It was fantastic," he said. "We put together a series of events and entertainments and marked every re-opening as an important step to recovery. It was always in my mind that the Trafford Centre would be opening quite soon. A lot of the people I represented had jobs in the city centre and I had seen their livelihoods disappear in a split second. It was a real imperative to keep shoppers and visitors coming despite the loss of some of the most popular retailers."

Paper blasted out of office windows litters the ground

Chapter Five

Sparks

IN the chaos of the immediate aftermath of the explosion,Chief Superintendent Peter Harris neglected to declare the event a Major Incident. While this would, of course, be stating the blindingly obvious, such a declaration does get certain things prioritised and contingency plans instigated. As it happened, everything was done correctly and Mr Harris is perfectly prepared to admit his one error on the most difficult day of his professional life.

The police established three concentric cordons – a wide outer ring to prevent traffic entering the city centre; a second up to a half-mile radius from the seat of the blast to prevent access to damaged property, and a third around ground zero itself. Within hours of the explosion, co-ordination arrangements were established which, according to the Home Office's study, *Business As Usual,* which details the action taken in Manchester as a valuable case study in responding to terrorist attacks, proved their worth during the following weeks. Twice a day a local co-ordinating group of senior council officials and police officers met to take stock of the situation and establish priorities. At least once each day the police and the council addressed large gatherings of owners and occupiers of buildings in the affected area. About 5,000 people came to the town hall for help and advice during the first weekend and a similar number attended each of the meetings during the following week. A team at the town hall worked round the clock staffing a business helpline, giving out information and meeting the need for counselling. The close working relationship established at all levels between the police and the city council secured the confidence and support of the business community as they could see that they were being kept informed and that everything possible was being done by the authorities to reduce the cordons in a structured way and to safeguard their property. Officials began the massive task of collating a catalogue of all the people whose cars remained trapped within the secure area or whose businesses had been left unlocked when the order came to evacuate and could not be reached.

The police and the city council made it a priority task to release buildings from the cordon as quickly as possible so that owners could gain access to premises, assess damage, carry out repairs and re-open for business as soon as possible. But public safety had to remain the prime consideration and falling glass presented a considerable hazard.

Despite the terror attack, the Euro '96 football match scheduled to be played at Manchester United's Old Trafford ground on the Sunday afternoon – little more than 24 hours after the bombing in the city centre, just two miles distant – went ahead. Thousands of German and Russian supporters walked to the stadium which had been closely searched and heavily guarded overnight. There had been a major question mark over the wisdom of staging the match, but the city's leaders were determined it should go ahead, not least to send a signal of defiance to the bombers that Manchester was still in business and terrorism would not win. More than 50,700 fans who packed the ground to its then capacity endorsed the sentiment. Four days later, when Germany played Italy at Old Trafford, the then German Chancellor Helmut Kohl was among the VIPs in the stadium's directors' box.

It was Monday before building control staff began slowly working inwards towards ground zero, making their assessment of the damaged areas as they went. Moreover a significant area of the devastation was designated as a crime scene and was likely to remain so for some time. Yet, as people coming to work for the first time since the blast encountered traffic congestion chaos caused by road blocks around the core area, there were few complaints. Mancunians took the calamity in their stride and got on with it. The affected area was divided into zones, each inspected for structural damage by a team of surveyors operating under the control of the City Architect. As each area was declared safe to enter, council workers were deployed to clear glass and debris and then the owners of the premises were allowed in. A strict pass system was operated to guard against looting.

Within 48 hours of the blast around 70 per cent of the properties which had initially been cordoned off had been released to their owners, and after six days only the most severely damaged buildings were still out of bounds. More than 600 vehicles were stranded in the city's car parks for five days because of damage to surroundings. Their release was controlled by police on proof of ownership.

Despite the speed of the operation, many members of the business community were upset and fearful for the future, especially traders bombed out of the Royal Exchange and Corn Exchange buildings close to the epicentre of the blast and destined not to reopen for months, or indeed, years. Leese recalled that there was an enormous number of people to deal with but running large meetings was something that politicians aren't bad at. The first was chaired by Pat Karney, who won the leader's praise for doing so very effectively.

Karney recalled: "It seemed everybody in business was heading for the town hall. There were huge numbers and it was apparent to me there wasn't a lot of experience on hand to deal with them. I'd been trained through the Labour Party to handle large meetings so I think I did the first seven. There were people screaming about their businesses; when they could go back in and so on. My message was that the city would be back on its feet and I was determined with all my colleagues on the council and all the other agencies to rebuild Manchester. That's what you have to say in such emergencies. But I meant it."

The overriding priorities were reassurance and confidence building as well as the establishment of a means of supporting small traders, many uninsured against terror attacks, until they could relocate and resume their businesses. The early pledge that Manchester would recover better than before from such a massive blow sounded like bravado, but Leese insisted his message was very much a statement of intent. The bombing had come as a massive shock and sparked an emotional reaction in him that he admitted he was still to feel ten years on.

"I'd walked past the point at where the bomb went off an hour earlier on my way from Victoria Station to the town hall that day. If there was a low point it was seeing the violation of where you lived. At the first council meeting soon afterwards I had a great deal of difficulty speaking about it. I broke off and started again. Keith Whitmore, then leader of the Liberal Democrat opposition, took over. But on the rebuilding pledge, from day one it was a real and deliberate statement of intent. It was never going to be easy but we never had it in our minds that we were not going to do this."

Howard Bernstein, the then deputy Chief Executive of the council, was also left reeling by the shock of seeing the centre of his home city in ruins. "The scale of the disaster only emerged when Chief Inspector Seabridge took me close to where the bomb had gone off," he said. "My first reaction was to wonder how it had been possible that no-one had been killed. That in itself was a miracle. But it was obvious that the position really was very desperate. I wondered how we would ever recover; I'd never seen such destruction in my life before. It all seemed pretty chaotic. Who was in charge? I remember Graham Stringer and Pat Karney pinning me to the wall in the town hall on the Sunday and saying: 'You've got to fucking sort this.' You move into a different gear then. All the shock and outrage subsided and I thought to myself that we had to do something about this, introduce some discipline and some good old bureaucracy. I'm nothing if not a good old bureaucrat, so we started to bring the process in and kept things going – basically by sitting in the town hall day and night."

One of Bernstein's first acts was to contact Tony Strachan, the Bank of England's agent in the North West and ask him to get all the bosses of the clearing banks in the city together. Bernstein went to Strachan's office where all the representatives of the banks were assembled and made an extraordinary request: an absolute commitment that none of the bankers in the room should foreclose on any business without reference to him.

Bernstein told them: "You must give me the opportunity to keep businesses going." Later he said: "I don't think anyone there could believe I'd asked them such a thing." But in an unprecedented show of solidarity they concurred, though Strachan did warn afterwards that financial institutions could not ignore ultimate financial realities.

At another meeting, Richard Leese, Howard Bernstein and Sir David Trippier the former Tory minister recently appointed chairman of the Manchester Airport-funded Marketing Manchester, received a standing ovation from assembled business people. Bernstein recalled: "I'll never forget that. Richard and I spoke to them about what we'd done over the past seven days and what we hoped to achieve. As we left the room, they clapped us. It was remarkable to see the business community applauding a Labour council leader and a town hall deputy Chief Executive like that. They knew who we were and there was an obvious feeling of mutual trust and respect between us and the private sector that I don't think you would have seen anywhere else in the UK."

The business helpline soon developed into a more substantial, broadly-based team comprising staff from the town hall and representatives of agencies like the Training and Enterprise Council, Business Link and the Citizen's Advice Bureau to provide general advice and practical support to small firms and individuals to help with recovery. But it wasn't enough.

Leese's optimistic words in the face of disaster had been echoed by the Prime Minister, John Major, in the House of Commons. "What's clear in Manchester, in the past and in the future is that there has been an effective partnership between the government, the private sector and the city council," he said. "This partnership provides an excellent basis for the rebuilding."

But there was no specific pledge of financial aid from central government, and businesses in the city – in particular the bombed-out small traders – were in dire straits.

On the Wednesday following the blast Manchester launched its Lord Mayor's Appeal Fund in the name of the city's current first citizen, Derek Shaw, to assist those who had suffered injury or loss and hardship in the explosion. The fund, set up by the city's Chief Executive, Arthur Sandford, swiftly became the focus of recovery efforts in the short to medium term and eventually distributed more than £2 million in grants and loans to around 700 applicants. The fund was administered by John Glester, the senior civil servant head-hunted from Government Office North West back in 1988 to become Chief Executive of the ground-breaking Central Manchester Development Corporation whose activities had been wound up in March 1996. Peter Heginbotham, a leading Manchester corporate and employment lawyer who served on the board of Manchester Enterprises for a decade and as President and later a senior director of the Manchester Chamber of Commerce and Industry also joined the Lord Mayor's Fund team.

Bernstein said: "Arthur was brilliant at the nitty-gritty and John was a bureaucrat par excellence. The fund was a remarkable achievement by people who had an incredible empathy with the city. The support they drew in from all the different agencies was instrumental in putting the city back on its feet."

When the dust had settled no-one had much of an inkling of the scale of help that hundreds of businesses would need. The lack of appreciation was unwittingly summed up by the production team at the Royal Exchange Theatre, who, on the afternoon of the day of the explosion reported to chairman Ken Harvey: "Missed the matinée but we should be on tonight." That was wishful thinking on an epic scale.

"Enormous numbers of people were getting in touch with the Lord Mayor and other council officials to see how they could help," recalled Glester. "There was an understanding that there needed to be some sort of emergency organisation to deal with pressing needs and so the appeal was born."

At the height of the crisis, the Lord Mayor's fund's administrators were taking just five days to process pleas for help from the appeal stage to the handing over of cheques. It wasn't enough to save some broken businesses, but almost 400 small firms were rescued from the ruins and 300 individuals offered vital assistance. Aid in kind from public and private sector sources kept the administration costs down to just one per cent of the fund's turnover. "Not many charities can demonstrate that," said Glester. "It's something the whole of Manchester can be proud of."

The project proved an invaluable life-raft for many businesses and received generous support from the business community. Two of Manchester's most distinguished adopted sons made massive contributions at an early stage; Sir David Alliance donated £200,000 and Sir John Zochonis' Charitable Trust gave £100,000, taking the fund past the psychologically reassuring £500,000 mark and maintaining vital momentum. Sir David, now the Liberal Democrat peer Lord Alliance, arrived virtually penniless from his native Iran and went on to found the international textile group Coates Vyella and become chairman of one of the UK's leading mail order companies. Both he and Sir John, the Imperial Leather soap magnate and patron of many organisations from the National Society for the Prevention of Cruelty for Children and Christie's Hospital to the British Museum, are among Britain's best-known and generous philanthropists.

Corporate Manchester weighed in with remarkable generosity. Marks & Spencer, despite its own grievous blow in the blast, gave £100,000, as did United Utilities. The Co-op donated £50,000 and the Ship Canal Company and Manchester Airport £25,000 each. Many more organisations gave in excess of £10,000 in a dramatic demonstration of a city's diverse strands all pulling together in time of need. People were more than ready to respond to the appeal; the Lord Mayor barely needed to ask.

Glester said: "We had pocket money from kids who sold toys at their garden gates, from ex-Mancunians living away and from local authorities all over the country. Touchingly, some of the donations came from places that had themselves suffered disasters. We wondered about a cheque from north Devon – and then realised Lynton and Lynmouth had suffered a terrible flood in the 1950s."

Central government's contribution eventually reached £300,000 but there were anxieties that the fund should not be seen as a replacement for insurance cover and that people who had not paid premiums should not derive an advantage over those who had. It made for delicate and complex interviews between staff seconded from banks and insurance companies and applicants for help. Few of the staff had much experience of the tales of trauma related across their desks and Glester admitted it took a special kind of person to cope.

He later revealed that at the first meeting of the fund's administrators a flat rate payment of £100 had been envisaged as typical; the average turned out to be around £15,000. Some applications for aid came months after the blast; the reason, Glester explained, was that some people had been so shell-shocked by their experience that they could not bring themselves to come back into the city centre any sooner.

Perhaps the most bizarre story in the days following the explosion involved 77-year-old Danny O'Neill who emerged, unhurt and relatively unshaken from his flat in Cromford Court – home to 75 people on the roof of the devastated Arndale Centre – three days after the blast. When the block's caretaker had knocked on the door on the Saturday to evacuate the close-knit, elevated neighbourhood, Dan, in bed with 'flu, had stayed where he was and simply turned over and went back to sleep after the bomb shook the ducks off the wall of his home. Staff in the office of the flats' owners, the Northern Housing Association, were stunned when he rang them and asked: "I'm feeling much better, what should I do?" His nonchalant shrug and comment: "You can overdo this danger business," summed up the Mancunian mood.

Later, it turned out, Danny had not been alone in remaining at home in the enclave when the bomb exploded. His neighbour Vera Featherstone, 58, who was running a bath when the caretaker sounded the alarm and didn't hear the call to evacuate, remained undiscovered for two days. "I had no idea that just a few yards away people were running for their lives," she said later. "I was enjoying a long soak and soon after I got dressed the front door blew off in front of my eyes and I ran for cover. I assumed my neighbours would return soon so I got on with washing my curtains and cleaning up the mess."

Most of the residents of Cromford Court – the block took its name from an old square that had been buried beneath the Arndale development - returned to their homes within a year and, with cash from the Lord Mayor's Fund, replaced their lost belongings. A small band of pioneers in city centre living, their stay would be short-lived; their flats demolished not by the bombers but to make way for the massive £100 million redevelopment of the Arndale North.

Barbara Welch, the Preston woman who had been the bombers most grievously-injured victim, also spoke for the first time – in fulsome praise of the emergency crews who rescued her and the doctors and nurses at North Manchester General. "I wish it had never happened, but my life has to carry on," she said. "The medical team have been superb. I could have asked for nothing better."

By Friday the local chart band 808 State were staging a dance party in the Castlefield Arena – scene of the mass gathering of Mancunians on the night of the 2000 Olympic bid announcement three years earlier, when the city refused to take no for an answer to its sporting ambitions and swiftly switched its target to the Commonwealth Games.

And the Royal Exchange Theatre Company, determined that the show was going to go on, announced plans to set up a temporary home at the Upper Campfield Market, off Deansgate, though for how long no-one at that time could speculate.

The city's immediate response to the disaster that had befallen it has been adopted as a template for others. According to the Home Office's case study in its 25-page document, subtitled "*Maximising Business Resilience to Terrorist Bombings: A Handbook for Managers*", the Manchester experience was "as educational as it was challenging". But at the time, the most important response from the point of view of the city's commercial future came with the arrival in Manchester, one week after the bombing, of the chairman of Marks & Spencer.

Sir Richard Greenbury headed what was, in 1996, the most profitable and powerful presence in the British high street, moreover one with long-established and deep roots in Manchester. Michael Marks opened his first store in 1894 in the front room of his home in Cheetham Hill Road and replaced it three years later with larger premises in Stretford Road which traded until 1933. In 1898 Marks – with Tom Spencer now on board - opened the first Manchester city centre store in the Upper Campfield Market before moving to 60 Oldham Street where they traded until 1925. Two more moves finally brought M&S to the newly developed site on the corner of Corporation Street and St Mary's Gate; the company's fourth biggest store in the UK and its regional headquarters.

Greenbury, a regular visitor to the city, not least to follow Manchester United, was out of the country when the explosion happened but on his return made it a priority to visit the damaged store and meet all the Manchester staff. The gathering at the city's Piccadilly Hotel was their first coming together since the blast. Human resources managers from several local stores also attended, recognising it was likely to be an emotional occasion and, for some, the loss of their work environment would be extremely upsetting. The chairman delivered a personal thank you to his 570 employees and promptly announced that Marks and Spencer would build a new store that would be "truly magnificent."

He declared: "M&S has traded in Manchester for 102 years and in 1994 we had a wonderful Centenary bash at Old Trafford. Manchester was one of the company's top four flagship stores in the country and it [the new one] is going to be 120,000 square feet of the most magnificent store anywhere. Let's be frank, you can replace bricks and mortar and the spirit showed by the people of Manchester is going to produce a magnificent city, better than before. Tragedy will be turned into opportunity." He drew a parallel with Sir Matt Busby, the legendary manager of Manchester United, who had no football ground after Old Trafford had been all but destroyed by an enemy air attack in World War II, but went on to produce one of the greatest of all teams.

Greenbury's statement of intent was talismanic. Richard Leese was in no doubt about the importance of Marks & Spencer's commitment to the city centre. "In 1996 Marks & Spencer was the flagship store in every high street and other retailers, when considering particular locations, had their judgment coloured by how close they were to M&S. The world has changed in ten years and Marks & Spencer has had its troubles, but back then it was vitally important, not only to us, but as the single most important confidence booster to the city's business community."

The stage was set for what Bernstein called "three years of absolute bloody hell – a roller coaster. We provided an opportunity for change that only a dynamic city could have done."

Leese added: "The rebuilding process was something like a three-year adrenaline rush."

Council leader, Richard Leese

Chapter Six

The Hunt

THE search for the bombers began an hour before their home-made device exploded. The moment the codeword was delivered to Bootle Street police station a pre-arranged set of systems clicked into action. There had been two previous IRA attacks on Manchester city centre and the police, anticipating a third, had contingency plans.

While the evacuation was still underway, the registration of the Ford Cargo van was processed through the Police National Computer database which produced a name and address in the south east for its registered owner. It was this first, simple connection that would eventually lead police to track down their suspects, though none of the bombers would ever face trial for the Manchester detonation.

As the countdown continued, Special Branch officers in Manchester were checking up-to-date intelligence on known Republican activists and talking to the Metropolitan Police Anti-Terrorist Unit.

In the Nineties, IRA bombers normally operated in teams rather than as individuals, with instructions for the active service units relayed from Ireland. Many Provos were known to the police and security services who monitored their activities. There was no point arresting them until it could be proven they were involved in a particular event, but silent surveillance was a useful tool in identifying their associates.

A man who was subsequently to become the chief Manchester suspect had been monitored by MI5 for months before June 15. Codenamed 'Paradise News' they tracked him while he lived at an address in London. They believed he and a number of associates were planning a simultaneous attack on power stations in the capital. The authorities were so sure that the threat was imminent that they employed 300 MI5 and police personnel in the surveillance operation, codenamed Operation Airlines.

It is unclear how many security personnel were watching him and his associates on June 14 and 15, 1996.

When the bomb exploded in Manchester the police had three avenues to explore. The first was forensic. What goes up must come down, and whatever was in that lorry – aside from a very large amount of fertilizer mixed with sugar which was atomised – was going to land somewhere in the city.

Eight years earlier, Pam Am Flight 103 disintegrated over Lockerbie, Scotland, while travelling at 31,000 feet with a ground speed of 434 knots. More than 10,000 pieces of debris from the bombed Boeing 747 were spread over a corridor 81 miles long, covering 845 square miles. The investigators painstakingly picked up every piece they could find, recognisable or not, and put it back together in the world's biggest 3-D jigsaw. Eventually, they found a 20-inch hole had been punched in the fuselage of the forward hold, causing a chain reaction which broke up the plane within seconds. The bomb had, they discovered, been in a Samsonite suitcase slipped on to the aircraft during a stop-over at Malta. A circuit-board from a Toshiba Bombeat radio-cassette player had been the trigger for the Semtex explosive. Baby clothes from the same suitcase were traced back to a Maltese manufacturer who identified a photograph of the man who had bought them. That man was subsequently found guilty of mass murder. All of that from 31,000 feet.

Forensic collection in Manchester was difficult, but far from impossible. It was just a case of manpower and time. They found bits of bomb and larger pieces of Cargo van on the ground, on window ledges, in shops and offices and on rooftops. Some debris was fired a mile into the sky but it did not spread out further than a circumference of a few hundred yards. Much was caught by the buildings it penetrated. The scientists would spend months behind their microscopes looking for traces of humanity, identifiable grains of soil, pollen and vegetation, anything that might begin to tell some part of the story of how and where the van was loaded with explosives, of its final journey and of its occupants. DNA evidence was in its infancy but samples from the inside of the van so small as to be invisible to the naked eye were identified and preserved.

The police have steadfastly refused to reveal precisely what they discovered in the unlikely event, that for whatever reason, the inquiry is re-opened in the future and they have to present it as evidence at a trial. Needless to say, forensic science has moved on significantly since 1996 and much more can be gleaned from samples than was possible then, but Greater Manchester Police refuse to say whether they have yet used modern techniques to study the samples.

The second avenue was CCTV. Today it is everywhere; in 1996 it was sporadic, but where it did operate was the motorways. Footage from every CCTV camera in the city centre was seized to try to establish what route the van took into the blast zone. Then every police force in the country and the Highways Agency were asked to preserve any footage they had from class-A roads and motorways on the Saturday and the two days prior so it could be viewed. The van could have travelled from anywhere, using any route, circuitous or direct.

The detectives tasked with watching the footage must have thought someone upstairs didn't like them. It was the most boring job in the world, staring at a screen, waiting for something that might be the van to flash by and then to check it again in slow motion, trying to see the number-plate. But it was vital. And they succeeded.

The camera network told them that on the afternoon of Friday June 14, the day before the explosion, the Ford Cargo was driven south along the M1 into London. At 7.40pm it was heading north on the same motorway in tandem with a Ford Granada. The two vehicles stayed together throughout their journey. Detectives made an educated guess that the van had been loaded with explosives in London and the Granada was the bombers' getaway car. This was an extraordinarily dangerous convoy. If there had been an accident, or if the primer had been set off by the motion of the vehicle, a section of motorway would have ceased to be and death would have been guaranteed for a lot of people.

Both vehicles were then seen at Junction 2 of the M6 in Coventry at around 9pm and again at Junction 10, Walsall, at 9.36pm. They then disappeared from view until the following day, probably garaged somewhere in north Staffordshire or south Cheshire. Police speculated that there was an IRA sleeper cell in the area. Nearby Warrington had been attacked twice – on the second, appalling occasion two bombs claimed the lives of two children – and the detectives on that case felt the killers had local knowledge or contacts with that knowledge.

The following morning another camera photographed the van at 8.17 on the M6 at Junction 19 near Knutsford, Cheshire. There are two ways into Manchester from there. The most direct and quickest is along the M56, past the airport and in through the southern artery. More circuitous is up to the M62, turning east and taking the M602 through Salford. The second involves more motorway miles and less A-road travel, and therefore less chance of being stopped at a random check which was always a possibility at a time of heightened security. The bombers took the second route.

The lorry was last seen moving east-bound on the M62 at 8.31am. Forty-eight minutes later it was photographed stationary outside Marks and Spencer's. Three minutes after that a parking ticket was slapped under its windscreen wiper as two men wearing hooded jackets and keeping their heads down got into the back of a Ford Granada and were driven away along Cathedral Street.

The knowledge that the vehicle had been driven south to London and then emerged from there on its journey north was utterly vital to the inquiry. The detectives knew that the Metropolitan Police were tracking a suspected IRA active service unit operating in the capital. The question was: had the London team hit Manchester?

The third strand for the investigators was technology. But by the time came for them to use it, the suspects were already caught in a police net.

The tracking in London by the Metropolitan Police and MI5 of known

IRA activist, 34-year-old Donal Gannon, had paid dividends. At an address he visited in Tooting, he was watched meeting up with 40-year-old Irish-American former marine John Crawley and a known IRA man, Gerard Hanratty, 38, both of whom had previously served IRA-related prison terms. Subsequently, an associate of Crawley's, Robert Morrow, led the surveillance team to two other known Provos who happened to be in town, Patrick Martin and Francis Rafferty. On July 9, three weeks and three days after the Manchester explosion, Gannon visited another address in Peckham, south London. Police raided it shortly afterwards and found evidence of a bomb factory in the shape of bomb 'housings' each designed to hold up to 3.8 kilos of Semtex.

On July 15, exactly a month after the Manchester detonation, all six were arrested. After a three month trial each man was convicted of conspiracy to cause explosions at National Grid electricity sub-stations and sentenced to 35 years in jail. The group was described as one of the most dangerous terrorist gangs ever to operate on the UK mainland and the convictions were said to rank among the most significant successes for the police and MI5 in the previous 25 years. Mr Justice Scott Baker told them: "You set out to destabilise the community by wrecking the electricity supply. You were reckless as to the number of people who might be killed or maimed as a consequence of your planned bombings. You did not succeed because the security forces were one step ahead of you."

Even before the men were arrested on July 15, work was underway to establish whether or not they were responsible for Manchester. Officers involved in the Manchester inquiry, codenamed Operation Cannon, traced the registered owner of the van who told them he had sold it to a dealer in Peterborough. That man told the investigation team that he had sold on the vehicle for cash to a Mr Tom Fox after a series of odd contacts.

The dealer had first been contacted about a different truck at the end of May. The man who called himself Tom Fox telephoned from a landline in Ireland and agreed to send £2,000 in cash by registered post in payment for a large van. The money never arrived. The sender contrived to put the wrong address on the envelope and the deal died.

Two weeks later, on Thursday June 13, two days before the Manchester detonation, Irish-accented Mr Fox rang the dealer again to make another purchase which was to be the Ford Cargo van. Arrangements were made for it to be collected the following day and paid for again in cash, but this time the money to be hand- delivered by a taxi driver. Once the payment was received, the dealer was to take the van to a local lorry park and leave the keys and documents hidden inside. On this occasion Mr Fox was using a mobile phone which would become central to the police inquiry.

Detectives set up a satellite incident room in Peterborough to follow all leads coming from there. Everything Mr Fox had done was now a priority. They were interested in his failure to send the money for the first purchase and, remarkably, the misdirected registered mail was returned by the receiver with the cash inside and turned up in a sorting office in the Irish Republic where it was seized.

Its sender's name and address were false but many of the 134 banknotes in the package had serial numbers which were very close to others later found at Gannon's London address. One note found in Gannon's wardrobe was just seven away in sequence from another in the £2,000 in cash sent to Peterborough by cab. Another from the same stash was consecutive to one recovered from the first Peterborough package that went astray. Gannon was now linked to Tom Fox, to both van deals, and therefore to Manchester.

It was in Peterborough that the technology became important. Police checked phone records and established that amongst inquiries to the Peterborough dealership, some had been made from a mobile phone whose subscriber lived in Ireland. The telephone, codenamed Digit Six because of its last number, was on an Eircell contract, but the calls had been made from the UK mainland.

It made four calls to the dealer, two from Manchester on June 13, two days before the explosion, and two the following day, first from Birmingham and then from Wisbech, Cambridgeshire. On that day, the geography of the calls suggested, the phone was being carried south. The police already knew the Cargo van had travelled from Peterborough to London on that Friday. The timing of that journey tallied with the timing and geography of the phone calls. This, they believed, was confirmation that Digit Six was linked to the Cargo van.

Detectives concluded the IRA unit had visited Manchester on the 13th to finalise their target and establish an escape route, then picked up the carriage for their terrible payload on their way back south.

Further inquires revealed the entire active life of Digit Six. It was first used in Ireland on June 2 and lastly in Manchester on the day of the explosion. It made 26 calls, mostly to relatives of its registered owner, all in Ireland up until June 10 and then, from June 12, in England. One number dialled was recognised by investigators as that of one used by a known IRA operative. It made two calls on the morning of Saturday June 15, first at 9.22 and then a minute later – three minutes after the bombers abandoned their device in Corporation Street having removed a clip attached to the primer, so starting the countdown. Detectives are certain the calls were to confirm the bomb was in place.

The phone was never used again and twelve days later, on June 27, its owner reported that it had been stolen on June 10. Generously, he paid the phone's total bill of £66.40, including the rental up to August, despite his report of it being stolen.

The evidence gained following the London arrests while circumstantial, was compelling to detectives. However, those at the top knew there were other matters to consider. First, the men were under arrest and no longer a threat, so would further charges be an unnecessary complication? Second, political, influences were afoot. There was talk of ceasefire and the potential for long-term peace. Would public pursuance of the Manchester suspects jeopardise that? Thirdly, and most importantly, their inquiries had unearthed the identities of a number of probable IRA operatives – one in particular - who were all now being secretly watched. Was it smart to move in on people in an action which would undoubtedly send the surveillance targets back underground?

Huge concrete slabs in the walls of the Arndale Centre were torn away

Chief Superintendent Peter Harris

The commander of Special Branch in Manchester, a Greater Manchester Police assistant chief constable and a senior officer from the Royal Ulster Constabulary met to consider their options. After a lengthy discussion they chose to keep many of their discoveries secret and not to carry out the normal procedure of informing the Crown Prosecution Service of their findings, effectively taking the lawyers out of the decision making process. The three departed the room promising to keep their pact totally secret. The specific reasons for their actions remain secret to this day but undoubtedly involved anti-IRA action being undertaken in Ireland at the time.

Two years later, in July 1998, circumstances had changed to such a degree that the three decided to release the full file to the CPS. However, the lawyers decided there was insufficient evidence to be reasonably certain of securing a conviction and no action was taken.

In April 1999 the *Manchester Evening News* got access to files on the case, published the name of the Irish suspect who was the alleged owner of the Digit Six phone and reported how he was watched by security services when he visited Manchester 18 months after the explosion, toured the site of the devastation, and was then allowed to return to his home in Crossmaglen, South Armagh.

In 2000 the Good Friday ceasefire agreement allowed for all IRA prisoners to be released from jail. The last of the men sentenced to 35 years for their roles in the London plot, Patrick Martin, walked free on July 28 - four years, one week and six days after the Manchester detonation.

Had he ever faced trial for involvement in the bombing of Manchester and had he been convicted, whatever sentence was handed down, he would still have walked free on that date and at that time. The agreement was all-compassing. Whatever had been done in the name of Irish Republicanism, however recent the crime, everyone was released. It was the price of peace, a price which could have been paid before June 1996 and before February of that year when a previous IRA ceasefire was ended with a murderous explosion at London's docklands.

Pictures of Patrick Martin and that of the other five men sentenced for the London plot were printed in the *Evening News* above a story claiming they were the chief suspects in the Manchester bomb. The newspaper has not so far been sued.

But if the process of bringing the bombers to justice was stalled for whatever reason, political or otherwise, their callous deed had set Manchester on course to unleash a decade of dramatic changes in the shattered city that might otherwise have taken 30 years to accomplish, erasing the blight of the previous half century along the way.

Chapter Seven

Dark City

THE post-Second World War years had not been kind to Manchester and, as in many other northern industrial cities, austerity lingered into the 1960s. Aside from the iconic Free Trade Hall, which was rebuilt and re-opened in the early 1950s after being almost completely destroyed in a German air attack, the city centre saw precious little in the way of major reconstruction until the dawn of the 1970s. And then, when the landmark Piccadilly Plaza, Arndale Shopping Centre and so-called Market Place were unveiled as exercises in concrete and yellow-tiled modernism, Mancunians did not much like what they saw. Indeed the exterior of the Arndale, then the largest indoor shopping complex in Europe, was said to resemble the biggest public convenience in the world.

The Clean Air Acts of the 1960s rekindled a local appetite for Victorian and Edwardian grandeur when the decades of soot and grime were sandblasted from the city's landmarks. The Mediaeval cathedral and Alfred Waterhouse's magnificent town hall re-emerged a honey-coloured limestone that hadn't been seen in living memory; the Midland Hotel glowed in rich, polished terracotta and the Central Library's Portland stone glistened white again. The architectural heritage of the world's first modern city that had "disappeared" during a century of blackened anonymity suddenly came to life.

The stark new-build looked ugly by contrast, but it could have been a lot worse. Manchester's immediate post-war planners envisaged a new city centre comprising serried ranks of Piccadilly Plazas encircled by four and six-lane boulevards, it's Victorian heritage bulldozed away; the town hall demolished to make way for a car park. Fortunately, the city was broke and the 1945 Plan survives only as an intriguing might-have-been.

There was no doubting, however, that Manchester was a city in steep decline. Employment in textiles, the industry that had given the city its nickname, Cottonopolis, had halved between the two world wars; from 1961 to 1983 the city lost 150,000 manufacturing jobs and between 1966 and 1972 a quarter of its factories and workshops disappeared. Within thirty years a third of the inner city population had moved away and those who remained suffered the upheaval of swapping slum conditions in clapped out pre-1914 terraced houses for the squalor of their system-built replacements in "Fort Ardwick", "Fort Beswick" and especially the crescents and deck-access flats of Hulme.

Between 1954 and 1974, Manchester demolished 90,000 homes and built 71,000, mostly on overspill estates several miles outside the city and as high-rise flats closer in. But this new world proved disastrous in social terms and was plagued by crime and isolation. Moreover, the speed and scale of the re-housing programme – by the late 1970s half Manchester's population lived in council homes - undertaken with stretched resources, resulted in blocks beset with structural problems, damp and poor insulation.

By the early 1980s the economic crisis afflicting Manchester took on a political aspect. Apart from a brief period at the end of the 1960s, Manchester had been Labour-run, but as the party fragmented nationally in the wake of Margaret Thatcher's General Election victory in 1979 and subsequent reforms, internecine strife also broke out at local level.

The city council, run by Labour's old guard, not only came under pressure from ministers bent on stripping back local authority powers and reducing grants, but from a new, young breed of left-wing activists whose politics had been forged on university campuses where bitter disappointment with the performance of the 1974-79 Labour government was commonplace.

Their leader was Graham Stringer, raised in Beswick in the heart of east Manchester's accelerating dereliction and educated at Central Grammar School - one of five state grammars in the city later turned into comprehensives - before graduating with a degree in chemistry at Sheffield University.

It was Stringer and his ally Pat Karney, chairman and secretary respectively of the Manchester Central Constituency Labour Party who, as early as 1979, first suggested politely to the sitting MP, Harold Lever, that it was about time he stood down. The fact that Lever, as Chief Secretary to the Treasury, had been one of the most influential figures in James Callaghan's Labour government, counted for nought. Margaret Thatcher had won the General Election and Labour was about to tear itself apart in the consequential blame game. Within the year, Lever had gone to the House of Lords and the left-leaning Bob Litherland was the new MP following the by-election.

Labour traditionalists who had run Manchester for decades, save for a brief Tory interregnum ten years earlier, were deeply suspicious of the new Bennite twenty and thirty-somethings who appeared on the scene in the early 1980s. They accused the new left of staging crucial meetings at "inconvenient" times and continuing them late into the night in order to grab key positions of influence, not least control of the Manchester City Labour Party and with it, the mechanism for selecting election candidates and writing the election manifesto.

Karney explained: "The young Turks had arrived on the scene, fresh out of university, and we went back to the places we were brought up; Beswick in Graham's case, Harpurhey in mine. We were a new phenomenon in the Labour Party and the old stagers didn't really know where we were coming from or how to handle us." Through the process of removing incumbents in favour of like-thinking activists, the Left faction increased its representation within a fundamentally divided controlling group on the city council. They in turn accused the old guard not only of managing decline, but co-operating with the Thatcher government and being prepared to give away council land to the private sector in desperate pursuit of economic development.

Stringer challenged for the leadership in 1982 but lost and there followed a bitter civil war which, at one stage, saw him expelled from the Labour group for life and most of his fellow travellers suspended for frequently voting against their own party in the council chamber. Out of sheer exasperation, Norman Morris, the Manchester University don who led the City Council at the time, complained bitterly to the party's National Executive Committee about the antics of Stringer's growing faction, but the outcome wasn't what he expected. The NEC despatched the left-wing Liverpool MP Eric Heffer – who later saw fit to demonstrate a show of solidarity with the Militant Tendency when it came under attack – to Manchester to broker an uneasy peace between the sides. Both staged press conferences accusing the other of treachery, but for the sake of relieving the party of chronic embarrassment, the hatchet was buried. The result of the 1984 local council elections, however, put the boot firmly on the other foot.

The tipping point came after the poll when candidate selection finally gave Stringer's faction the whip hand within the Labour group. When the councillors met to elect the group's officers, Stringer, who had failed two years earlier, gained his majority. He assumed leadership of the council at the age of 33 with a radical social and economic programme certain to set the city at odds with the Thatcher government.

Their early excursion into gesture politics included the scrapping of the Lord Mayor's trappings; the fur-trimmed scarlet robe, 18th Century-style feathered tricorn hat and elaborate, gilt and enamel chain of office were confined to an obscure town hall locker. The elegant Lord Mayor's private apartments, furnished with antiques and commanding panoramic views across Albert Square from the fourth floor, were closed, but an attempt to abolish the office itself, was blocked – first locally by an alliance of Conservatives and Labour's old guard in the council chamber, then by the realisation that it would take an Act of Parliament and the Sovereign's consent to do it. The Queen's picture was taken down from its place of prominence opposite the town hall's splendid Great Hall. The lofty ceiling inside the massive, chandelier-hung hall with its famous original paintings of scenes from the history of Manchester – some rather fanciful – by Ford Madox Brown, was painted with the coats of arms of the British Empire's former dominions. Those of South Africa were covered over by the flag of an African nationalist movement. It remained there even after Nelson Mandela was released from his long imprisonment. Only later was it realised that the black and red banner wasn't that of Mandela's African National Council at all, but the flag of the South West African People's Organisation (SWAPO) who had fought the apartheid regime's forces in neighbouring Namibia years earlier.

The assault on the office of first citizen was later described by Stringer as a "propaganda disaster". Karney, concurred. While Stringer was relatively taciturn and lugubrious, Karney was frequently the mouthpiece of the new administration with a fine line in strident political sarcasm. "They said I was gobby," he recalled. "I was aware of that and I had an appreciation of the importance of the media, something Graham learned from me."

The media, however were not exactly appreciative of Karney, especially the "equality agenda" that he took upon himself to espouse. The town hall's new regime established a Police Monitoring Committee, with Karney in the chair, bringing themselves into conflict with the Greater Manchester force's then Chief Constable, the controversial but populist James Anderton. And, like their counterparts in Ken Livingtone's left wing Greater London Council, they expressed empathy with Irish republicanism and foisted gender issues on to a Manchester general public that was not, Karney admitted later, anything like ready for it.

"We did things that I greatly regretted later, but you have to realise how young and idealistic we were, mostly in our 20s and early 30s, and very new to local government. Some of it was madness. Gay and lesbian groups would not meet in the town hall because they said they felt it was oppressive so we booked hotel rooms for them and rubbish like that. We had a gay and lesbian flower bed in Piccadilly Gardens. I can't believe we were so out of touch with the Manchester public; it makes me cringe with embarrassment."

History tells us that many such ideas were simply ahead of their time and a lot of the issues are now mainstream, but Karney conceded that back in the mid-1980s the Labour group had created a lot of own goals in terms of the way they handled them.

The surviving pillar box became a Manchester icon

All the glass in the roof of the Corn Exchange was smashed

Offering a council job to a Sri Lankan asylum seeker, Viraj Mendis, while he was holed up claiming sanctuary in the Church of the Ascension in Hulme also attracted stinging public criticism. It seemed bizarre that, Mendis, a revolutionary communist who had overstayed his entry permit and claimed he would be killed if he was returned home, should seek the protection of Mediaeval church laws from the authorities. It didn't work; he was eventually deported after police stormed the church. He survived and later made his home in Germany.

"I can remember being out canvassing with Stringer on the doorsteps in north Manchester and having to spend thee-quarters of an hour on each one explaining why lesbian and gay rights were priorities and why we'd replaced the Lord Mayor with something called a chair of the council," said Karney "Our own supporters didn't know what we were talking about. How we first got involved with all that I've really no idea. It gave Norman Tebbit [the Conservative Party chairman who branded Labour councils 'the Loony Left'] and the hostile tabloids a field day."

For all the radical – and slightly ridiculous - posturing, however, what set alarm bells jangling in Westminster and among private sector interests in the North West was always the new regime's determination to implement a publicly-led investment programme at the same time as trumpeting a "no cuts, no redundancy" policy despite diminishing resources.

Years later, Stringer was ready to admit there was no realistic hope of carrying through those ambitions under a Thatcher government. The logic therefore dictated that the most productive way forward was to strike an alliance with Arthur Scargill's National Union of Mineworkers and municipal socialists in other cities, which would make it possible, if not to bring down Thatcher, to at least force a reversal of policy that would provide money for house building and investment programmes. It was, to all intents and purposes, a revolutionary stance.

The prospect was not viewed at the time as the forlorn hope that hindsight suggests; when the Left's policies were being formulated, the NUM's two victories over Edward Heath's government in the 1970s were still fresh in the memory. Led by the doughty Wiganer, Joe Gormley, the miners walked out on strike in January 1972 in pursuit of a pay claim. Within a month the government was forced to impose a three-day working week on industry to conserve coal stocks but power cuts nevertheless plunged the country into darkness. By the end of February, the government capitulated. When the NUM imposed an overtime ban in November of the following year, Heath immediately called a State of Emergency and three days later the miners voted for an all-out strike on February 4th 1974. The Prime Minister called a snap election on "who rules" and narrowly lost, leaving Harold Wilson leading a minority Labour government.

Initially, as Prime Minister, Margaret Thatcher shied away from confrontation with the miners, who in 1981 again balloted to strike, this time over the government's plan to close 23 pits. The Department of Energy retreated and agreed to reduce coal imports in response to the NUM's demand that no collieries should be closed for reasons other than exhaustion. But Thatcher was merely biding her time and when the inevitable clash eventually came in 1984, the government was ready.

Moreover, while Liverpool's Militants were at first believed by their Manchester counterparts to have achieved moderate success with a radical house building programme in 1982, they dramatically overplayed their hand by threatening, and eventually carrying through, an illegal policy of refusing to set a budget. The rebellion on Merseyside not only earned the condemnation of the Conservative government but eventually that also of Labour's leader Neil Kinnock. In his impassioned "Black Taxi speech" to Labour's 1985 conference in Bournemouth, Kinnock railed against left-wing factions within Labour ranks that he believed were making the party increasingly unelectable. The Militant Tendency, with its own newspaper and outspoken Liverpool powerbase – a party within the party - was the most obvious target for the forthcoming purge. Kinnock's outburst, delivered without warning, was electrifying.

"I'll tell you what happens with impossible promises," he boomed. "You start with far-fetched resolutions. They are then pickled into a rigid dogma, a code, and you go through the years sticking to that, out-dated, misplaced, irrelevant to the real needs, and you end in the grotesque chaos of a Labour council - a Labour council - hiring taxis to scuttle round a city handing out redundancy notices to its own workers".

Karney, himself very much of the Left, was nevertheless shocked at what was being done by the Militant regime in Liverpool, fronted by the populist Derek Hatton. "We went there in early 1984 and what we saw frightened us to death," he recalled. "We'd always adopted a softer stance; there had been a series of secret meetings with David Blunkett who was council leader in Sheffield at the time, and we'd taken more inspiration from Ken Livingstone's Greater London Council, like monitoring the police. Being products of our time, we thought that the Thatcher years would be short-lived, but she won her landslide in 1983 then again in 1987. It was so depressing some people were thinking of going abroad."

By the end of 1985, the game was virtually up. In March of that year, after twelve months of increasing hardship and ugly violence, pitman against pitman, the miners' trickle back to work became a flood and the NUM called off the strike. It was a comprehensive defeat; the elite of the Labour movement was shattered and demoralised.

The defeat of the miners, however, failed to quell the rebellion in Manchester town hall. Graham Stringer's ruling left-wing faction had resolved to follow in Liverpool's wake and refuse to set a budget in 1985. The council was only prevented from outlaw status by the combined votes of the Labour old guard and the Conservative opposition and a budget was eventually set that relied heavily on the using up of reserves to finance their policy of maintaining service and employment levels at the town hall. The following two years saw the deployment of a series of creative accountancy ploys such as deferred payments and the lease and lease back of many of the city's assets, including the Central Library and the Wythenshawe District Centre.

Frances Done, a member of the city council since 1975 but a close ally of Stringer, became chair of finance in Manchester's new, left-wing administration in 1984. She was instrumental in implementing the novel "creative accounting" schemes aimed at reducing the city's overall budget which, in the labyrinthine system of local government finance at the time, attracted bigger grants from central government. "The system doesn't work like that any more," she said. "But in simple terms, if you managed to get the budget below a certain figure, you got more grant. The figure in my head is about £80 million, so there really were quite substantial numbers involved."

She was later to become Treasurer and Chief Executive of Rochdale Borough Council and then Chief Executive of Manchester 2002, which delivered the Commonwealth Games and for which she was awarded a CBE. In November 2003 she became Managing Director of the Audit Commission for Local Government. Given her background, as she puts it, "on all sides of the fence", it was an inspired appointment.

The council set up the stand-alone Manchester Mortgage Corporation which, financed by loans from foreign banks, leased several major council-owned assets then leased them back to the city. The lease and lease back idea was controversial and unusual but, Done insisted, perfectly legal, though opposition politicians in Manchester and in Westminster were deeply suspicious about the scheme.

She said: "I was a politician and chair of finance, yes, but I was also an accountant and absolutely not someone who would go and do something I thought was irresponsible. I particularly would not have been party to anything which would have meant we would spend lots of money now and someone would have to pay for it over the next 20 years. That wasn't how the deal was at all. The money brought in by leasing and leasing back the assets was put safely away and the interest on it was used to reduce our budget. I'm not sure now where the ideas originated, but they would have been supported at the time by Peter Short, who was City Treasurer and Roger Taylor, the Chief Executive. Neither man, for whom I have the greatest respect, then and now, would have ever supported a scheme of live now, pay later, and don't worry what happens in ten years time. They would have given a great deal of careful consideration of how to use what were novel financial arrangements to the benefit of the council without causing any damage."

The aim, according to Done, was to buy time and ultimately work towards a stable, balanced budget. Unlike some of her council colleagues, Done did not believe that the election of a friendlier Labour government at the General Election of 1987 would have suddenly opened the way to a far more generous local government grant settlement than Mrs Thatcher's Conservatives were prepared to contemplate.

"What we were attempting was to manage the budget towards stability while still maintaining council services," said Done. In her mind that did not mean carrying on regardless of costly inefficiencies - tantamount to blasphemy in Labour's heartlands during the mid-1980s; moreover, her drive towards delivering services closer to the people at neighbourhood level – ironically now the mantra of David Cameron's new model Tories – was threatening to cut across the government's rules requiring compulsory competitive tendering. The prospect that the council's own departments would lose contracts to private-sector service providers was beginning to cause rumblings among the town hall trade unions.

In the end Manchester's financial tightrope act was unbalanced by the Conservative government's blunt instrument; the rate cap restricting councils to set limits on the amount they could raise by local taxation. It meant that in March 1988, following a 20 per cent rate rise the year before, the city was saddled with a potential deficit exceeding £100 million, it was clear that time – and money - had finally run out.

Frances Done did not stand for re-election in May 1988 and returned to her accountancy profession with the leading firm KPMG, not, she admitted later, without some anxieties. Despite being adamant that the creative accounting schemes deployed during her stint as chair of finance were above board and would cause no long-term damage, Done recognised that suspicion had lingered.

"I was very aware personally that I was regarded a bit as damaged goods in the financial world," she admitted. "I had been associated with a very controversial scheme which I knew was not harmful to the city, but explaining that to anyone who wasn't directly involved was nigh on impossible. In the end I contacted a senior partner at KPMG and asked to see him. I explained that things had become tricky around my reputation, but I wanted my job back and I returned to the firm for three years before going off to Rochdale."

The Tory victory at the 1987 General Election when Margaret Thatcher secured her third successive term, once more with a Commons majority of more than 100 seats - despite a well-received campaign by Labour's leader Neil Kinnock - was a body blow to Manchester's administration and Stringer and his colleagues were staring into a financial abyss.

There could be no rescue by a grateful Labour government, just the prospect of financial meltdown and the bleakest of political choices: U-turn or rebellion, with the risk of dire consequences both personally for councillors and for the city as a whole – of the sort that later became only too apparent in Liverpool. There, 47 councillors were surcharged to the tune of thousands of pounds each and disqualified from office, and the Labour Party was banished into opposition. In terms of the momentum of regeneration, the city fell at least a decade behind Manchester.

Richard Leese, Stringer's successor as city council leader, admitted: "In the early 1980s there was this notion that municipal socialism could take on the government and win. What we found out was that although municipal socialism could take on the government if it wished, it could not win. It was a learning curve for a lot of people who were comparatively young in local government terms – in their early 30s – with little experience."

Leese, born in Mansfield, had worked as a teacher in Coventry before arriving in Manchester as a youth worker at the council-run Abraham Moss Centre in Crumpsall, to the north of the city centre. Within two years of becoming a member of the council in the revolutionary year of 1984, he had become Chairman of Education and later took the chair of the Finance Committee. A lot of people had gone into fairly senior positions very quickly without a great deal of experience. The leading lights of that group were all from working class backgrounds, he recalled, but had a middle class upbringing – in other words, a state grammar school education following selection by the 11-plus examination that was largely swept away by the comprehensive system but remains one of the biggest controversies dogging Labour to this day.

He said of Thatcher's 1987 triumph: "There was no get out of jail card. We had gambled on Labour winning the General Election and we lost. It meant, with the rates capped, we would have to make really deep cuts."

With Manchester's socialist experiment to all intents and purposes at an end, Stringer despatched a letter to the then Secretary of State for the Environment, Nicholas Ridley, saying, in a nutshell; Okay, you win; we'd like to work together with you.

"It was a very straightforward letter," Stringer recalled. "I can remember getting it out years later and showing it to friends after John Major had come up with £55 million for Commonwealth Games facilities and saying 'this is where all that started'. It wasn't quite rolling over to have our tummy tickled, but it was the recognition that we'd not accepted after the Tories won the 1983 General Election that we had to have a relationship. Ridley never responded but his officials understood the significance of the letter and when he was replaced by Chris Patten at Environment our willingness to co-operate was recognised and it was further cemented by Patten coming to Tokyo for the 1996 Olympic Games decision."

Stringer's letter of capitulation came at the end of a major debate within the Labour movement in Manchester. Though the controlling group on the council had stuck to their "no cuts" pledge between 1984 and 1987, it had become inevitable that the cuts would now have to start. Councils that refused simply put their heads on the block.

Stringer said: "We had a huge debate which began immediately after the General Election in June and lasted until the end of July. I went round every constituency party and every trade union branch in Manchester. One of the biggest meetings was in the Free Trade Hall; the place was full. I did nothing for six weeks apart from try to convince the membership that we had to recognise that we were not going to turn the government over and we would have to look at private capital, European funding and central government money – the Lottery came much later – for extra resources. We were never going to get back however many tens of millions the government had taken away from the city by reducing grants, so we had to change our policies."

He managed to carry the vast majority of the council's Labour group with him, but confessed later that steering though what amounted to a spectacular U-turn, day after day, at a series of sullen ward party and trade union branch meetings was the most difficult five months of his life. Effectively, Stringer burned his boats during those weeks; there could be no going back. In retrospect he conceded that had he not been able to carry the argument, he would have resigned as leader – or been sacked.

"Back in 1985 the unions and the city Labour Party were in favour of illegally refusing to set a budget, but we were voted down in the council chamber. But times had moved on. I wouldn't have remained leader by my own choice or by others' choices had I lost the debate because I had argued so strongly for making cuts and defending whatever services we could. I believed it was the only way of carrying on with our radical agenda – it's no longer radical of course – on equality and anti-discrimination issues, gay rights and all those sorts of things, because if we'd gone illegal and been disqualified as councillors, as happened to the Liverpool Militants, all that would have gone as well."

In the end, the result wasn't even close. Stringer carried the day at the largest ever meeting of the key city Labour Party – the body that selected candidates and produced the policy manifesto. Of around 185 delegates packed into the meeting, only 20 or so voted against the new strategy of co-operation. Every single constituency Labour Party and trade union branch signed up.

"By the time the vote took place," said Stringer, "most delegates had been mandated to vote with us and when it came to the vote in the council chamber, one or two members of the Labour group might have abstained or voted against, but once the party as a whole had made its decision, it was very difficult for the few dissenters to hold out."

Nonetheless, Stringer was subjected to bitter criticism from his former allies on the left. One scathingly described him as being "the man who led the revolution, then the counter revolution".

Sam Darby, the housing chairman who later challenged Stringer for the leadership, accused him of "bottling out". And his former deputy leader, John Nicholson, who remained a firebrand of the Left, was one of the first to shout "betrayal". Nicholson contended that the Conservative government had only allowed Labour councils to get away with their creative accounting schemes until the miners had been defeated; then it was to be the turn of the town halls.

Leese said: "Though we changed course, the internal debate rumbled on for the remainder of the 1980s and into 1990-91. During the era of the poll tax there were people wanting to repeat what we attempted in 1985." Despite strident protestations over the unfairness of the poll tax, there was no rebellion; time had moved on and Manchester was recognising the benefits of its much-modified political stance. Stringer dismissed the now marginalised left-wing voices within Manchester's Labour group as "a few romantics".

Chapter Eight

Into the Light

GRAHAM Stringer's letter of capitulation to Nicholas Ridley was met with a deafening silence from government - yet that moment signalled not only the beginning of Manchester's remarkable renaissance but also, long before anyone had heard of Tony Blair or Bill Clinton's arrival in the White House, the birth of New Labour and the Mancunian Third Way.

Nevertheless, if Manchester's Labour leaders expected any reward for executing their 180 degree policy switch, dyed-in-the-wool Thatcherite Nicholas Ridley was not in a giving mood. A strident right-winger, he became Environment Secretary in the reshuffle after Michael Heseltine stormed out of a Cabinet meeting and into the political wilderness following his bitter disagreement with Mrs Thatcher over Westland, the UK-based helicopter company. Heseltine, the Defence Secretary, favoured a European rescue package for the struggling helicopter manufacturer; Thatcher wanted Westland to merge with the American company, Sikorski. Angry that his views were being ignored, Heseltine walked out.

Ridley was hardly in the business of patronising socialists. And the government's imposition of an urban development corporation upon central Manchester was a clear indication that the council was not to be trusted despite the apparent new-found willingness, at least on paper, to co-operate. The decision was aimed at deliberately shutting out local left-wing politicians from the regeneration process of a large and important swathe of the city centre.

The government could hardly be blamed for its attitude. As Richard Leese later admitted, Manchester's Labour leadership was not shy of co-operating with the private sector simply because they feared corruption - the equation: local authority + big business = T Dan Smith. Smith, the ambitious leader of Newcastle city council had been jailed for six years for conspiracy and corruption in 1974. It was much purer than that.

"I don't think anything like that entered our heads," he said. "There was never any particular concern about corruption; we were all puritans. Discomfort about working with the private sector actually sprang from the ideological view that capitalism wasn't a good thing."

The UDC initiative earmarked for Manchester was not strictly Ridley's idea, but a policy legacy left by the interventionist Heseltine from his time at the Department of Environment earlier in the decade. By 1987 there were already a number of UDCs - designed specifically to stimulate private sector investment in areas of dereliction. The first two had been set up by Heseltine in London's Docklands and on Merseyside after the Toxteth riots, followed by others, not least in Trafford Park, the huge industrial estate to the west of Manchester which was in steep decline with the shedding of traditional manufacturing jobs.

The task of establishing the new Central Manchester Development Corporation fell to David Trippier, MP for Rossendale, who had become Minister for Inner Cities and Construction in the post-1987 election reshuffle.

Michael Heseltine

His task would not be easy, for the council's leader, Graham Stringer and his colleagues were deeply hostile towards the idea from the outset. Nor was business interested in co-operation with the city's left wing politicians during what councillor Pat Karney later – only partly joking – came to characterise as their "Chinese period"; his tongue-in-cheek description of the attitude to the private sector that was prevalent within the town hall at the time.

Trippier was unaware of Stringer's surrender letter to Ridley and expected to confront major difficulties ahead from a resentful Manchester. Opponents of UDCs saw them as the heavy hand of government descending from on high to impose a strict autocratic framework on the development of the economic and physical environment. The idea was to stimulate the necessary energy to bring public and private sectors together and act as a

Sir David Trippier RD, JP. DL

catalyst for change that otherwise might not take place for a considerable time, if at all. Moreover the minister knew that whatever powers central government may have had, they could be effectively neutered without the support of the local authority. And vice versa; local councils would not be able to deliver major improvements without the support and financial assistance of government.

Trippier said: "The simple fact that central and local government need each other as an essential ingredient for the recipe for success was clear to me when I was the leader of Rochdale council and I had to work with both Labour and Conservative governments." But he was convinced that "absolutely nothing would happen" without the private sector having the confidence to invest.

And the going was tough. He later admitted that it was only the fact he was an unqualified supporter and devotee of local government that stopped him "sticking his head in the gas oven" out of sheer frustration in dealing with some inner cities and the politicians who ran them.

In Manchester, frustration might well have been the least of his worries. There were two major obstacles; the council appeared ideologically opposed to co-operating with either the private sector or a Tory government they had been committed only a short time before to trying to bring down.

To Trippier, whose career had started in the family stockbroking firm and who had been recently appointed Honorary Colonel in the Royal Marines Reserve in the North West of England, Manchester in 1987-88 appeared a basket case, both politically and financially.

"The council was trying to find miraculous ways of getting itself out of debt," he said. "They were even thinking of leasing off the town hall square. When that appeared in the press I think it sent a bolt of lightning through the business community right across the North West. For a time the mayoralty was, to all intents and purposes, abolished in favour of a council chairman. I remember him, Ken Strath – and I remember Prince Philip coming and saying 'Who's that?' because the Lord Chair, as he was laughingly called, was wearing a Labour Party tie and CND badges down the front of his jacket.

It was quite amusing in one sense, but I could see that if we weren't careful, my city was going to go down the pan and in fact it wouldn't have taken very many years for it to have followed Liverpool.

"The Lefties even got rid of the military silverware from the town hall. I believe it went to Tameside and when Manchester eventually asked for it back they were told to fuck off. Manchester really was like a banana republic; the town hall, which wasn't a priority, became extraordinarily scruffy and there seemed to be crèches all over the place."

In his 1999 memoirs, *Lend Me Your Ears*, Trippier was brutally frank. "Although the words partnership and confidence are synonymous with Manchester today, it was not always thus. The ideological tripe which was peddled by those on the far Left, may, for a time, have convinced a few zealots who were against us being a democratic nation with a mixed economy. For that same length of time, however, nothing – but nothing – positive happened."

No wonder that, in the beginning, the relationship between minister and council leader was strained. The pair were like chalk and cheese; one an urbane and well-groomed Tory, used to glad handing and working rooms at society and business gatherings; the other a rather awkward, casually-dressed, earnestly resolute left wing political bruiser, more at home amid the confrontational turmoil of Labour's legendary smoke-filled rooms, though Stringer himself, unlike Tripper, was never a smoker.

Nonetheless, the ability – and more importantly the willingness - of the two men to find common ground and do business was pivotal to Manchester's recent history.

Trippier recalled: "He complained that I kept giving money to Salford but nothing to Manchester. I said, of course – Salford was prepared to work with the private sector and Salford Quays, on the site of the old Port of Manchester, was going to be a great success. On one occasion at the end of a year when I had some of my budget left over to allocate, I rang the chief executive of Salford, pulled him out of a council meeting, and told him I was giving him another £1.5 million. It got into the paper – we wanted it to. Graham wasn't best pleased but I said to him: 'Salford's more Labour controlled than Manchester is, but they will work with us'. The worst thing that ever happened to Salford was when Graham and Manchester saw the light."

Stringer's position was that Manchester required government money to carry through a publicly-funded regeneration programme. Trippier told him: "You haven't done it and you cannot do it on your own".

Despite the early tensions, Trippier is generous in his book as to Stringer's role, crediting him as being the man who led Manchester out of the shadows. "I was simply one of the people who were in a key position at the time and who made him face reality," he wrote. "Graham didn't have to read the tea leaves to tell him what was going to happen as he had seen Salford make great strides with the private sector. He had also seen what had happened in Liverpool as a result of Derek Hatton declaring a fortress policy which was hammering the Merseyside economy and driving the private sector away. And he had seen that I would not give government assistance through the City Grant I had created unless the private sector was in the lead and calling the shots.

"He had also seen that the Urban Development Corporation I was setting up in central Manchester was inevitable. Things had to change and, to his eternal credit, he changed. A man of immense intelligence and integrity, he moved his position not by a whisker but by 180 degrees. Despite our political differences, which will never be reconciled, we shared a deep affection for Manchester which ensured we were able to work together and bury the political hatchet for the sake of the city and its future.

"I might not have had a loud voice," Trippier recalled, "but I had a big stick: the chequebook."

Richard Leese said: "What we learned, and very quickly, was that despite the assault on local government from central government there were still real things that we could do for the people we represented and, to a certain extent, a lot of that did not relate directly to the powers we had or even the budget. It was developing an understanding of the leadership role a local authority could play in an area by working with a whole range of other people, including the private sector. I think the ideological issue that guided us at the time was based on relatively simple logic.

"The phraseology comes from the early 1990s when I wrote papers for the Party: What was the biggest problem Manchester faced? Answer – poverty. What were the biggest causes of poverty? Unemployment, low skill, low wage employment. Therefore, if we were going to address poverty, a pre-condition of that was the creation of jobs and, certainly in the late 1980s and early 1990s, it wasn't going to be us creating the jobs, it was the private sector."

Early meetings between Stringer and Trippier were conducted in private, which Trippier said was unusual, since ministers usually required a civil servant to be present as a "witness". But after the second get-together Trippier realised "this was a man I could do business with". The minister insisted that there could be no access to City Grant - the new all-embracing central government fund for local authorities - to finance projects unless the private sector was in the lead, hence the necessity to impose a UDC. Stringer retorted that if the UDC was imposed, he would personally attack Trippier in the press.

"I understand that," replied Trippier. "You do what you must do. And when you've got that off your chest, I'd like you to go on the UDC board. Stringer said, 'you're joking aren't you?' and I said no, I'd rather work in partnership with you than be at loggerheads. I am prepared to have the UDC delegate the planning administration – the back office stuff – to the city council."

Stringer was taken aback by the offer and didn't give an answer straight away; but then he agreed to join. The Development Corporation's remit did not embrace the whole of the city centre, but a crescent-shaped area from behind Piccadilly Station, through the Whitworth Street corridor and round to the Granada TV studios, hard against Manchester's boundary with neighbouring Salford.

When he saw the map, Stringer told Trippier: "You haven't included the

Free Trade Hall". The minister had considered the building in Peter Street to have such iconic status in Manchester's political history – it was built on the site of the Peterloo Massacre of 1819 when a meeting demanding universal suffrage was charged by cavalry, sabres drawn, leaving eleven dead and 400 wounded – that common sense had told him to leave it out.

Trippier revealed: "Graham said: 'If you don't put that in, I can't get any money for it'." Stringer, even at that stage, had high ambitions to build a new concert hall home for the Hallé – later brought to fruition with the construction of the Bridgewater Hall – and wanted to realise a council-owned asset worth around £4 million. The Free Trade Hall had been restored during the years of austerity following World War II, but was in a serious state of disrepair. "I simply rubbed out the line on the map and moved it," said Trippier. "That's how business was done." Then, also at Stringer's behest, he added land opposite the Piccadilly Station approach which included the Joshua Hoyle Building, a derelict cotton warehouse later successfully transformed into the Malmaison Hotel. Ironically, Trippier's instinctive caution over the Free Trade Hall proved correct, if premature by almost a decade; when plans were unveiled years later for the conversion of the building into a luxury hotel, they sparked a major controversy.

Chapter Nine

Strange Bedfellows

GRAHAM Stringer's dealings with David Trippier over the Free Trade Hall were an indication that the council leader was not as averse to doing business with the private sector as he had appeared. The behind the scenes deal-making between left-wing council leader and a string of leading north west businessmen – including John Whittaker, the reclusive Isle of Man-based boss of Peel Holdings – would not only have raised an eyebrow in Westminster, but also within Stringer's own radical Labour group.

Though 1987's election result was the pivotal moment, triggering the profound political changes that were to shape Manchester's future, Stringer had been on a learning curve about working hand in hand with some of the region's key private sector players virtually from the start of his time in office, though few realised the implications. And it all began with the audacious suggestion that Manchester should bid for the Olympic Games.

As early as October 1984, when he arrived back in Manchester from the Labour Conference in Blackpool, Stringer received a message that Bob Scott was seeking a meeting. Scott, a diplomat's son who had acted in the West End, had arrived in Manchester in 1967. He launched the revolutionary Royal Exchange Theatre on the vast former trading floor and was credited with saving Manchester's two other major theatres, the Palace and Opera House.

Stringer remembers his first meeting with Scott vividly. "I'd gone to Marks & Spencer's to buy a new pair of trousers just before it," he recalled. "I'd been to the Labour conference in Blackpool and addressed a few fringe meetings and someone had spilled a pint of bitter over them. They smelled like a brewery."

He had imagined that Scott would be seeking an extension to one of the theatres, but the impresario instead stunned the council leader by suggesting that Manchester bid for the Olympics. Scott had been impressed by the Los Angeles Games, entirely funded by private business, and believed the demographic of Manchester was similar to Los Angeles.

"People thought I was an absolute lunatic but it grew and grew," Scott said later. Stringer listened intently, though Howard Bernstein, by then the city's deputy Chief Executive, confessed: "I thought Bob Scott was bonkers at the time."

It was relatively easy for Stringer to square the idea with the city Labour Party by saying it would probably be a good thing and anyway, the bid would involve no commitment of scarce public funds. In the event, the following year, despite Manchester being first with the idea, the British Olympic Association nominated Birmingham as the bidding city for 1992 and the Games eventually went to Barcelona. Nonetheless, a hare had been set running for future Olympic bids and, ultimately, the triumphant staging of the Commonwealth Games. But just as important was the germination of the seeds of partnership that would serve Manchester right up to the present day and particularly after the 1996 bomb.

Scott introduced Stringer to a number of key business players whom he otherwise would not have met, and a strategy for co-operation began to emerge in which the roles of public and private sectors were very clearly defined. Stringer summed it up thus: "We'll do what we need to do in terms of planning; you present proposals to government and raise the money. We gave the private sector a freedom they certainly didn't get in Birmingham during their bid process and they'd not had previously in Manchester."

Stringer's private sector contacts were also boosted by the city council's historical involvement with the Manchester Ship Canal Company which it had rescued from financial collapse while the cut was under construction in the late 19th Century. The death of its chief civil engineer, Thomas Walker, before its completion in 1894, coupled with continuing structural difficulties, prompted a withdrawal of the massive undertaking's backers.

The council stepped in with £5 million to see the project through, taking in return a majority of directorships on the board. By the mid-1980s, however, that arrangement had become meaningless, for although the city council controlled the company's board by statute, the millionaire property developer, John Whittaker, controlled virtually all the shares.

Remarkably, given their backgrounds, Whittaker and Stringer sat down and negotiated a deal which in effect saw the city relinquish all but one of its eleven seats on the Ship Canal Company board in return for a multi-million pound investment commitment in east Manchester which, almost 20 years later, is continuing.

They were the strangest of bedfellows, the left-wing political firebrand and the acquisitive capitalist, and stranger still, their relationship not only went virtually unnoticed by the media, but by most of Stringer's ideological socialist purists on the city council.

Stringer had come to realise that the town hall's Ship Canal Company directorships were not only a historical leftover, albeit a bit of a perk, but could potentially lock the council into an impossible position. And he was determined to extract a price for them. There were eleven council seats on the company's board and ten directors representing Whittaker's growing property firm, Peel Holdings, and it had become obvious that the shareholders' best interests would be served by developing land owned by the Ship Canal Company at Dumplington, close to what is now the M60 circular motorway, as the biggest out of town shopping centre in the UK. Such a course – the establishment of a major retail competitor to the city centre - was definitely not, maintained Stringer, in the interests of Manchester.

"I could see that we would have been locked into making a decision in favour of the development eventually because it was obviously in the interests of the shareholders," said Stringer. "I think John might well have taken legal action against us to make us vote that way. I don't think this conversation ever took place in these terms between John and me, but I think it was understood.

"You pay us a lot of money to relinquish our directorships – more than they're worth because otherwise we'll be a bloody nuisance within the Ship Canal Company – and we'll carry out our own interests on behalf of the city council, which are clearly not the same as yours. You carry on trying to develop Dumplington, because that's your business and we can have an honest disagreement about this rather than having conflicts of interest all over the place."

The "honest disagreement" eventually went all the way to the House of Lords before Whittaker overcame the legal opposition mounted by Manchester and other neighbouring local authorities to the shopping centre scheme, realised as the Trafford Centre, but the straight talking proved productive. "I think the position was understood all round but it didn't stop the fact that every time I had a pint or a glass of wine with John Whittaker he would tell me at great length how good the Trafford Centre would be for the centre of Manchester and I'd tell him how bad it would be and we'd exchange statistics," said Stringer.

"He's a passionate man who really believes in what he's doing. We might have been chalk and cheese but we did and still do get on well. He disagreed with our view on Dumplington and he didn't really understand politicians, but he saw we were honest about the way we were going about things. He respected the fact we weren't trying to mess up his business from the inside and he paid a very high price for that at the start. He took a risk but in the end it turned out to be a very low price when the Trafford Centre came to be developed."

The price the city council extracted for relinquishing its theoretical control of the Manchester Ship Canal Company was, in fact, £10 million, a considerable sum 20 years ago. Seven million was paid in cash and Whittaker guaranteed that his investment in Ship Canal Developments, a joint venture company with the council, would be worth £3 million after a period of years. The joint company, conceived as a vehicle for injecting Whittaker's capital resources and development expertise into depressed east Manchester, is still at work.

As chair of the town hall's finance committee at the time, Frances Done had been close to the negotiations between Stringer and Whittaker, but was aware of potential political pitfalls, not least within the council's Labour group.

"I personally thought John Whittaker was really good, but I couldn't have gone on the telly and said so, could I?" she recalled. "We had to make sure we got the best value out of our involvement with the Ship Canal for the city. We weren't stupid; we had to get the maximum leverage. Graham and I also worked very hard to ensure that the top end of the canal didn't get closed, which was absolutely the right thing to do. It was only because we were so bloody minded in public with John that it didn't happen. He couldn't proceed because he knew there'd be a lot of opposition."

In private, however, dealings with key private sector players like Whittaker were far from bloody minded, but the Labour group had little inkling of the growing relationships. "At that time any dealings with the private sector would have been regarded with suspicion," said Done. "In dealing with John Whittaker we understood the name of the game and I personally thought his takeover of the Ship Canal Company was a good thing because the previous board had not appreciated the potential for jobs and development. It was not a problem dealing with someone who's got enterprise and initiative in his approach, but it was tricky in that every move of every individual was being scrutinised by the Party.

"The external view was that as a group we were completely out of control, but the leadership knew exactly what it was trying to achieve. I personally never told a lie or did anything to mislead, but you had to find a way of dealing with the outside world, given the relationships that existed with the council officers and the Labour group and all the complications that went with that. It was very important with regard to all the things that came later because people like Robert Hough of Peel Holdings and Sir Alan Cockshaw of AMEC would later play major roles in the regeneration of the city. I must say it's all a darned sight easier now.

"A lot of trust was built up through straight talking behind the scenes between people you wouldn't imagine you'd have a relationship with in the first place. Had it been known it would have gob-smacked a lot of people and caused an awful lot of trouble within the Labour Party with a few purists who couldn't see beyond their ideology to the reality that is that you can actually benefit the citizens by behaving in a slightly different way."

There was a third strand to Stringer's learning curve about how capitalism worked, which led even more directly to what happened after the IRA's attack, ten years later. Manchester's new left-wing leaders were fearful that the Thatcher government's appetite for privatising public sector industries and utilities would eventually gobble up municipally-owned Manchester Airport. The Stock Market flotation of gas, electricity and telecommunications all proved popular with the public and lucrative for the Treasury. Manchester's legal attempt to secure some compensation for the city that had built the pioneering aqueducts to bring clean water from the Lake District reservoirs of Haweswater and Thirlmere to its cholera-prone population was brushed aside when the water industry was privatised. The British Airports Authority, operator of London Heathrow, Gatwick and several provincial airports, also duly passed into the private sector.

Bizarrely, Manchester's leaders sought to avoid the privatisation of its airport by devising a scheme to place it in the private sector themselves - via a company wholly controlled by the ten Greater Manchester authorities that owned it. And so it remained for eight months until March 1986, when the airport was returned to the public sector after it had been granted designated status under the 1985 Airports Act and the immediate threat of privatisation by the government was deemed to have receded. At the same time Stringer sought to mirror his deal with the Ship Canal Company's bosses by establishing Ringway Developments with £12 million, a joint venture company with the private sector, seeking to encourage airlines, aviation and related industries to set up in and around the airport. It is still a source of regret to Stringer, former chairman of Manchester Airport, that despite the huge expansion via second and third terminals and a second runway, it has no dedicated airline, like BMI's base at the much smaller East Midlands Airport, but the enterprise was to prove crucial.

Manchester advertised for partners and found banks and property companies willing to be involved. Most important of all, AMEC, the major construction company led by Sir Alan Cockshaw, came on board. It was the start of a long and extraordinarily fruitful relationship between council and private company, spanning many of the major projects of the following two decades, including the regeneration of Hulme and the conception of the City of Manchester Stadium, home to the Commonwealth Games and now Manchester City FC. Sir Alan, raised in a council house in nearby Swinton, later became the natural choice to chair the task force charged with rebuilding the city following the devastation wrought by the 1996 bomb.

David Trippier, who also invited Stringer's fellow Labour councillor Jack Flanagan to join the board of the Central Manchester Development Corporation, recognised the pressures on the council leader; he'd been there himself as the leader of Rochdale council in the mid-1970s. But once the respective political posturing had been gone through, each recognised they could do business with the other. In public they swapped critical comments in the press. Stringer accused Trippier of being instrumental in denying Manchester government funding; Trippier damned Manchester for its litter-strewn streets. But in private, said Trippier, they never fell out and neither let the other down.

Trippier remains fulsome in his praise for Stringer's achievement and leadership skills, and the two men have remained friends despite their contrasting backgrounds and political party loyalties. Of all the local authority leaders that Trippier met in his varying ministerial roles, Tourism, Small Firms and Enterprise; Inner Cities and Construction and Environment and the Countryside, he singles out Stringer as by far and away the most intelligent of the "new breed" of city bosses who emerged in the 1980s.

"After our initial difficulties we got on well. No-one would have believed it," he said.

In his memoirs, he wrote: "I did not realise at the time that his acceptance of the need for partnership would develop in such a dramatic way and the growing success of the city today owes much to the fact that he displayed so much vision and commitment while he was leader of the council. It was almost as if he'd invented the word partnership himself. Even so, I will always claim that I was the one who attached two jump leads to fire him up and point him in the right direction.

"He certainly required no further help from me, as he worked tirelessly to achieve great things for the city. I only hope that Tony Blair recognises his ability and he soon becomes a minister."

Trippier wrote that final paragraph in 1999; in fact Stringer did achieve brief ministerial rank in the Cabinet Office during Blair's first term, but rose no further. Trippier is not alone in wondering why such an analytical political talent – moreover one rarely prone to rebellion - should have been consigned so early to the back benches.

Howard Bernstein, the town hall's deputy Chief Executive when the CMDC was established, maintains that the image of the Stringer administration

Sir Howard Bernstein

as anti-private sector was flawed from the beginning; rather they were "pro-communities". The new wave of Labour councillors led by Stringer had brought a fresh awareness of what was right and what was wrong with Manchester.

"They were people of vision and leadership and I think Manchester had lost that," said Bernstein. "The city had not adapted well to the economic changes of the 1950s, 60s and 70s. In the 1980s we began to understand what our strengths were; the airport was a fantastic asset and the potential of the regional centre was huge. There was a recognition that successful cities had constantly to reinvent themselves."

Bernstein said from the outset he had been given every encouragement to work closely with Greater Manchester's Passenger Transport Authority to bring forward the first private railway in the UK for half a century, the Metrolink light rail system which replaced trains on the busy Bury and Altrincham commuter lines and linked the routes together through the streets of the city centre.

He conceded there was a body of opinion within the Labour ranks at the time that the council should not co-operate with the Conservative government, but not doing so would have been a gross dereliction of duty and responsibility.

"Yes, there was a political decision taken here but what were we to do, spend the next five years posturing?" he asked. "We were here to do the best possible deal for the people of Manchester with any government of whatever persuasion. Governments come and go as do their policies. We have to consider those policies and ask ourselves 'does it help us take this city forward to where we want to go?' There has never been a slavish doctrinal association with this government or that."

Nonetheless, despite having rejected the Thatcher government's view that local authorities could not be trusted to deliver physical and economic change in major cities, Manchester was forced to recognise that it was the Development Corporation or nothing.

With the city eventually on board, Central Manchester Development

Corporation - chaired by Dr James Grigor, seconded from a senior post at Ciba-Geigy, and with senior Government Office North West civil servant John Glester as chief executive - opened for business in 1998 with a budget of £101 million.

The mutual trust on which both Trippier and Stringer laid such emphasis had quickly become a feature of the council's relationship with the CMDC too. Not only did Stringer accept his seat on the latter's board - albeit at first, Trippier later acknowledged, to protect the council's position – but before long the CMDC was contracting out its planning functions to the town hall.

Stringer said later: "Jimmy Grigor was good because he knew the CMDC couldn't work without the city council's co-operation, [the acknowledgement was, in fact, mutual] so we worked very closely together. There was full integration between the two organisations; government kept checking whether or not we were doing the right things and Jimmy Grigor kept reassuring them that we were not loonies."

In the eight years of its existence, the Development Corporation, with its council and private sector partners, laid the foundations for a burgeoning city centre resident population with the conversion of warehouses along the Whitworth Street corridor into apartments, and oversaw the remarkable regeneration of Castlefield from decaying warehouses and a festering canal basin to an urban heritage park where apartments now fetch up to £500,000. Jim Ramsbottom, a former bookmaker whose vision was to reinstate the buildings in the area, some dating back to the earliest years of the Industrial Revolution and built on the banks of the world's first commercial canals, applauded the arrival of CMDC and its mission of supporting entrepreneurs with public subsidy. "They rolled into town on a white charger with saddlebags full of money and hit the ground running," he declared.

The most enduring legacy of the co-operation between the city, the CMDC and a now very much engaged private sector, is the Bridgewater Hall. It proved to be a vital overture ahead of the dramas to come, not least the Wagnerian episode of the bombing itself.

With the condition of the Free Trade Hall deteriorating rapidly and the council unable to finance major works, provision of a new home for the world-renowned Hallé Orchestra and two other orchestras, the BBC Philharmonic and Manchester Camerata, had been an aspiration since the 1950s. Notwithstanding the Free Trade Hall's place in the city's political history, it was hopelessly ill-equipped to meet the rising standards of service and acoustic excellence being demanded by musicians and concert goers alike.

In the new spirit of partnership, the CMDC acted as the catalyst that would deliver the dream with a viable and unique financial solution. Neither the European Union nor the UK government was making regeneration funds available for cultural projects, least of all for what would be Britain's first stand-alone international concert venue since the completion of the Royal Festival Hall on the south bank of the Thames 37 years earlier in 1951.

The key to unlocking access to the £42 million required for the new, 2,400-seat hall was the assembly of a creative private-public sector funding package dubbed the Great Bridgewater Initiative that would not only deliver the world-class concert venue but 350,000 square metres of much-needed prestige office accommodation around what was to become Barbirolli Square.

Sir Howard Bernstein said: "I don't underestimate the Bridgewater Hall as a major symbol of civic leadership. It wasn't just the fact that we built it, but the demonstration that we could conjoin the private sector in the delivery of the vision. Barbirolli Square was the most radical development that, in commercial terms, had ever been seen because it, in effect, moved the commercial centre of the city 500 yards down the road and that was a pretty sensational move at the time.

"A small step for mankind, if you like, but a giant leap for Manchester. The effectiveness of partnership between the city council and the private sector was demonstrated conclusively. At the end of the day, that's what developed the strategy we adopted, and the council's approach to the massive development of the business district around Spinningfields more than fifteen years later, and just about everything else in between."

It was clear that CMDC's objectives reflected the city council's aim to create a world-class regional capital and that Labour in Manchester – which ironically had tightened its political hold on the council – had successfully forged a partnership with a government-imposed organisation that had created new wealth and 5,000 new jobs in the city. It was a situation that a once wary private sector recognised too, and the council's reputation for being an agency with a strong and consistent leadership that could get things done in support of entrepreneurial activity was secure. But if Manchester's relationship with central government post-1987 had been pragmatic, the fall of Margaret Thatcher in November 1990, enabling the return to high office of Michael Heseltine, ushered in an era of much closer co-operation.

Chapter Ten

Brightness

MARGARET Thatcher's determination to reclaim Britain's big cities for the Tories - expressed on the stairs of Number 10 Downing Street at the hour of her third General Election triumph in 1987 - wasn't just manifest in the creation of quangos like the Central Manchester Development Corporation aimed at excluding Labour councillors from key decision making. She went much further. Her ambition to replace local government finance with a new Community Charge or Poll Tax was aimed squarely at divorcing councils from their so-called "client states" – voters who did not pay any rates, thus for whom "spendthrift" town halls were of no personal consequence.

The principle that everyone paid was supposed to bring the wrath of highly-taxed electors down on profligate councillors, overwhelmingly Labour, but it spectacularly backfired.

Manchester sent a large contingent of protestors to London for the anti-Poll Tax demonstration that turned into a full-blown riot on the eve of its introduction on March 31, 1990. Despite widespread opposition, Thatcher refused to compromise and its unpopularity, together with rising interest rates and emerging divisions within the Conservative Party over Europe, played a large part in her downfall.

The challenge to her leadership was precipitated by the resignation of Foreign Secretary Sir Geoffrey Howe after a particularly virulent Thatcher attack on Jack Delors, President of the European Commission. Howe openly invited "others to consider their own response" and Michael Heseltine, exiled from the Cabinet since his Westland walk-out, threw down his long-awaited gauntlet. Famously, Thatcher failed to secure outright victory in the first ballot by just two votes, was persuaded she would not win on the second, and stepped down. Though Heseltine was beaten for the Tory leadership, and by extension, the premiership, by Thatcher's favoured candidate, John Major, he was immediately invited back into the Cabinet by Major in his former role as Secretary of State for the Environment.

Graham Stringer, who by then had been leader of Manchester City Council for more than six years, still sees Hezza's reinstatement, and particularly in that role, as an absolutely crucial development in Manchester's recent history. And Heseltine was now a man in a hurry. Barely a month after his comeback he sought to keep a meeting with the leader of Leeds city council pencilled into his pre-ministerial diary. The Secretary of State was anxious to find out what was happening in local government prior to his dismantling of the community charge and subsequent re-introduction of a property based levy, the council tax. Heseltine was particularly interested in northern local government where opposition to the poll tax had been amongst the fiercest and asked his private secretary, Phil Ward, to get in touch with the leaders of other big cities.

By one of life's strange cross-party political coincidences, Stringer had been best man at Ward's wedding – the two had shared a room when they were at university – and a one-to-one meeting was arranged between Manchester's council leader and the Environment Secretary. The two-hour get together was extraordinarily productive, as were others that followed. Stringer gave Heseltine a résumé of Manchester's second bid for the Olympic Games that had been presented two months earlier by Chris Patten, then Secretary of State for the Environment, at the 9th Session of the International Olympic Committee in Tokyo on September 18th.

Manchester had this time won the backing of the British Olympic Association as Great Britain's representative and challenged for the right to stage the games in 1996 against Belgrade, Melbourne, Toronto, Atlanta and the sentimental favourite, Athens, where the first modern Olympics had been staged 100 years earlier. Significantly, in the light of later assertions that only London could mount a credible British bid, Athens was one of only two capital cities in contention; in the event neither won – the 1996 games went to Atlanta. Manchester's eleven-vote tally in an opening round that saw Belgrade drop out dwindled to five in the second and the city was eliminated at that stage.

Sir Bob Scott, Manchester's high-profile bid ambassador, later described the city's attempt to secure the 1996 Olympic Games as a "toe in the water job. We were like lambs to the slaughter and pretty ignorant, but it was a tremendous learning curve."

Howard Bernstein, whose sporting enthusiasm begins and ends with Manchester City Football Club, saw the adventure as a crucial step. "It all became very real after Tokyo," he said. "And the person I give real credit to is Chris Patten. He was absolutely convinced that the Tokyo experience wasn't just an extravaganza but a real opportunity to promote the UK abroad and urban development and urban concepts back home - and Chris conjoined government in that process."

It had made bidding for the 2000 games a very strong requirement to take forward the regeneration opportunities that the process would present for the city, even though the Millennium was not considered "Europe's turn" to stage the Olympics.

"The thing I never understood about the Olympics," said Bernstein, "was that when it was supposed to be Europe's turn in 2004, we didn't bid."

Despite the disappointment in Tokyo, Stringer and Bernstein convinced Heseltine of the merits of using sport as a powerful regeneration tool and spelled out Manchester's determination to try again for the 2000 games. Bernstein recalled: "At first Heseltine didn't understand it at all; then he shouted 'I love it, I love it' and we got £70-odd million for the site, the Velodrome and the bidding process." The money ultimately became the basis for capital investment in the Commonwealth Games venues, which in turn provided the bedrock for East Manchester's post-industrial regeneration programme, one of the biggest in Europe.

But that wasn't all. Heseltine had always taken a close interest in the state of England's big industrial cities, the more so when several erupted in rioting in 1981. The troubles flared in Brixton, south London, and most violently of all, in Toxteth, Liverpool, and it was there that the Merseyside Development Corporation was established and delivered landmark projects like the restoration of Albert Dock.

But Manchester had its riot too – at the gates of Moss Side police station, less than a mile from the vast council estates in Hulme, by the early 1990s sunk into a desolate crime-ridden virtual no-go area, completely beyond rescue. In his autobiography, *Life in the Jungle*, Heseltine spelled out his determination to tackle urban deprivation by encouraging effective local partnerships between public and private sectors and his readiness to reward councils who were prepared to co-operate. The result was the launch of City Challenge, for which local authorities with large areas of deprivation in their areas were invited to bid for £37.5 million of funding over five years by setting out detailed proposals for achieving their objectives. Essential to the bids was the endorsement of the plans by the local communities concerned, as Heseltine believed that without their support implementation would be meaningless.

The challenge was met with predictable opposition from many other Labour councils who scented a political fix. They were right, but not in the way they thought. Manchester's leaders had uttered routine misgivings publicly but had sent encouraging messages in private to the Department of the Environment; it was if the whole City Challenge scheme had been tailor-made for Hulme, and when the winners were announced in July 1991, Manchester was among them.

The Hulme initiative rekindled the relationship between Manchester City Council and strategic partners AMEC, led by the inspirational Sir Alan Cockshaw. Following an early career in both the public and the private sectors, Cockshaw had joined Fairclough Civil Engineering in 1973, becoming chief executive in 1978 and a member of the main board of the Fairclough Construction Group in 1981. After the acquisition of the Press Group by Fairclough in 1982 and the creation of the AMEC Group, he became Group Chief Executive in 1984 and Chairman of AMEC plc in 1988.

Under his leadership AMEC grew to become one of the largest engineering and construction companies in Europe, with annual revenue in excess of £2.7 billion and more than 25,000 employees world wide.

Cockshaw recalled: "I was asked to look at Hulme by Graham Stringer who was concerned about the amount of council resources going into the area which was bleeding other areas dry."

Richard Leese, then deputy leader of the council, vividly remembered when AMEC executives first unveiled their ideas for what the new Hulme could look like at a meeting attended by himself, Stringer and Dave Lunts, the city's housing chairman. The same group met again at Manchester Airport, this time with Michael Heseltine, and presented the model with its mix of social and private housing to him. "It's one of those things you can never prove, but shortly after that, City Challenge as a concept was announced," said Leese. "The City Challenge was almost a response to Hulme; it fitted the circumstances of the area perfectly."

The rebirth of Hulme, just a mile from Manchester city centre, is now internationally acknowledged as an exemplar of successful regeneration. The pump-priming £37.5 million of public funding attracted more than £200 million in private investment over the five-year programme which transformed the notorious and stigmatised area of high-rise and concrete deck access council homes into an integrated series of vibrant mixed-use, mixed-tenure neighbourhoods. The Hulme estates, though built only in the early 1970s, represented "old Manchester" at its worst. A survey in 1975 revealed that 96 percent of tenants wanted to leave the notorious crescents, and the city council, after moving families to other parts of the city, used them for housing young childless couples, single people and students. It didn't work; by 1986, 69 per cent of adult males in Hulme were unemployed. The area had become an impoverished wasteland, built around the crescents – four rotting hulks overflowing with rubbish, cockroaches, thieves and drug addicts. Its population had dwindled from 70,000 in Victorian times to fewer than 8,000.

The huge renewal programme – exemplified by the demolition of the crescents, which with cruel irony were named after a quartet of Britain's most noted architects, Robert Adam, John Nash, Charles Barry and William Nash – exceeded Heseltine's highest expectations and demonstrated the willingness of Manchester's Labour leaders to bury any lingering ideological objections to working closely with the private sector and, for that matter, a Conservative government. Heseltine duly took note.

Moreover, it saw the deployment of a new factor – the Hulme Design Guide, produced by the town hall's planners but very much influenced by the city's political leadership, which set out in clear, robust terms to developers, planners and residents what was required in terms of quality and expectation. Howard Bernstein said of the initiative: "The guide gave us all a clear understanding about what worked and what didn't work and Hulme was the classic example of telling us things that didn't work. At one level this is simple stuff but at another level it was quite revolutionary." The crescents, the walkways in the sky, and the crime infested cul-de-sacs had proved a social disaster and would never be repeated.

Leese admitted some mistakes were made but, armed with the design guide, steadily the council learned. He explained: "The first housing plan presented by developers was horrible and we said 'no', which was very difficult to say because they had done lots of work with tenants who thought the presented plan was wonderful. So there was a lot of work done to justify why we didn't want that particular form of development. But the point is, we learned all the time."

With City Challenge producing admirable results in Hulme, the drive to regenerate east Manchester, blighted by the collapse of traditional heavy industries as well as poor housing and consequential joblessness, low education attainment, poor health and rising crime, became the city's top priority. This was a sprawling district whose engineering factories like Beyer Peacock, Crossley's, Richard Johnson & Nephew and Manchester Steel had enjoyed international repute but had now vanished, leaving an industrial wasteland. Bradford pit had closed in 1968, Stuart Street power station, which it served, barely survived for another decade. The violence that accompanied the ten-month strike and workers' occupation prior to the shut-down of Laurence Scott and Electromotors' Openshaw plant in 1981-82 – one of the last major employers in the area – was illustrative of mounting local desperation in an area almost ten times bigger than Hulme and more problematic.

Heseltine promised that after the 1992 General Election – given a Tory victory, which was by no means certain - to set up a huge £80-£100 million urban development corporation there, but the scheme was one of the first casualties of Black Wednesday, the economic crisis that engulfed the government in the wake of Sterling's ejection from the European Exchange Rate Mechanism. As a consequence, getting funding into east Manchester by investment in sports facilities became not merely important, but essential.

Chapter Eleven

Going for Gold

WITH Manchester again receiving the backing of the British Olympic Association ahead of rival contenders including London, Birmingham and Sheffield, the campaign for the golden prize in 2000 was deadly serious business, notwithstanding the scepticism of much of the London-based media. The bid leaders really did believe their slogan, "We can win", and in vital ways, they did.

Manchester once more mobilised the big guns in government and private business to support the bid. Key to mounting a credible prospectus was the promise to provide world-class sporting facilities, but this was by no means just an ego-tripping sporting agenda; the buzz words were urban regeneration, employment opportunities and land reclamation amid the industrial dereliction of east Manchester where 60 per cent of the economic base had been lost between 1970 and 1985. It was almost as if the venues themselves would be by-products of the city's snowballing ambition to reinvent itself.

Howard Bernstein said he saw the bid as having several clear outcomes. "One was that it set us on a path of strategic planning and direction focused on how we could create a new role for east Manchester so that it could make a real contribution to the functioning of the city. That gave real impetus to our regeneration ambition by taking us to another level. The second outcome was that the bid would demonstrate our capacity not only to enjoy working with our respective private partners and the community, but we were also able to convince central government that here was a city they could do business with; one that had a strong vision about how it should reinvent itself. And it was a vision based on realism."

The first facility to rise amid what had been grandly designated SportCity – in reality the reclaimed, decontaminated spoil heaps of Bradford pit and the cleared site of Stuart Street power station – was the Manchester Velodrome, later renamed the National Cycling Centre. It was developed as a joint venture between the Sports Council, Manchester City Council and the British Cycling Federation and funding was provided by the government, through the Department of the Environment (£6.5 million), the Sports Council (£2 million) and the Foundation for Sport and the Arts (£1 million) with Manchester City Council as the freehold owner. Its 250-metre state-of-the-art track, the first purpose-built indoor cycling facility in the UK, is housed beneath a roof structure which provides an unrestricted viewing area for spectators. Since it opened in September 1994, many world records have been broken there and it hosted the 1996 World Track Cycling Championships.

On Christmas Eve 1992 work began in the city centre on winching away the cast iron and glass train shed over Victoria station to make way for the biggest indoor sports and concert arena in Europe with a capacity of almost 20,000. On a dreary wet day in July, 1993, members of the International Olympic Committee, led by its President, Juan Antonio Samaranch, and including ex-King Constantine of Greece, arrived on the site by Metrolink tram to view progress on the proposed Olympic gymnastics venue. So too had John Redwood, of all people, later John Major's right-wing challenger for the Conservative leadership, when he delivered the biggest City Grant ever awarded - £35.5 million – towards its construction cost of £56 million. The balance was met from private investment, with a further £2.5 million donated by the European Economic Development Fund.

Sir David Trippier, by this time a Minister of State in the Department of the Environment, remembered the occasion ruefully. "Just before the 1992 General Election we were being asked for an absolute fortune for the building of the Manchester Arena. I have to say that we had a ministers' meeting – the Environment department was so big there were seven of us with Heseltine in the chair – and I realised to my intense discomfort that I was the only one with a constituency north of Watford. When Heseltine said 'this [Manchester's grant application] is an awful lot of money', I told him that from a political point of view we couldn't not do it because there were a lot of marginal seats around Greater Manchester. We had two of the Bury seats and two of Bolton's. So I said how stupid are we going to look if we don't give this support – and it went through. At the end of the day that's how politics works, and that's why I never understood why the Labour government played fast and loose with the extension to the Metrolink tram system."

Trippier was referring to the Labour government's pledge to grant funding of £520 million to the so-called "Big Bang" extension of the Metrolink system over three new lines to Manchester Airport and Wythenshawe, Oldham and Rochdale, and to Tameside. But when costs spiralled beyond £900 million, the Transport Minister, Alistair Darling, pulled the plug on the project. Following an intense lobbying campaign by North West MPs of all parties, business interests and local councils, the £520 million promise was restored but, as the tenth anniversary of the IRA bomb approached, the widening funding gap had not been bridged.

Ironically, though the Tories triumphed for the fourth successive time in 1992, Trippier lost his Rossendale seat, a victim of pent up local anger over the poll tax despite his mentor Heseltine's dismantling of it as the Major government's first post-election priority.

The Manchester Evening News Arena, as it is now, officially opened on 15th July 1995 and has hosted major concerts and entertainment events. The arena was also home to the Manchester Storm ice hockey team, and still holds the European ice hockey attendance record of 17,245, for a Storm game against Sheffield.

During the IOC's visit, Samaranch, always the canny diplomat, declared in public that Manchester's 2000 Olympic chances were "very, very high". The bid team was jubilant at the endorsement, but realistic enough to recognise Sydney as clear favourites. Doubts were raised over the Beijing bid and Brasilia was expected to be dismissed early from the running. Bob Scott, chairman of Manchester 2000, said: "We've been striving for technical excellence and the report shows this has been delivered. The report shows that Manchester has a very strong bid."

Centrepiece of the bid – and principal of SportCity's regenerative programme – was the plan for the main stadium, a grand design by Arup earmarked for 50 hectares of reclaimed land in east Manchester. The original concept was for an 80,000-seat athletics-only stadium, striking for its sweeping roofline and mast and cable support structure. The Olympic prospectus envisaged an adjacent warm-up track and further sports facilities nearby. Though the stadium was never built in this form, the proposal became the eye of the storm over England's future national stadium to replace clapped out, 70-year-old Wembley.

Manchester also played its airport card. Since being perceived as under "threat" of privatisation during Margaret Thatcher's regime, it had gone from strength to strength. London's three airports at Heathrow, Gatwick and Stansted, together with a number of regional airports under the control of the British Airports Authority had been duly sold off, but Manchester, though converted to a plc, remained in municipal ownership; the city having 55 per cent of the shareholding and the remaining 45 per cent divided between the nine other boroughs that made up the former county of Greater Manchester, abolished by Thatcher, along with the GLC, in 1985.

Opened in 1938, the airport, then named after the village of Ringway, handled 7,600 passengers in its first fourteen months of operation; by 1987 the figure had risen to one million per month and when Terminal 2 was opened in 1993, capacity was increased to 20 million passengers a year. Its rail link was completed the same year and work on the second runway started in 1997. Manchester International Airport was a major backer of the Olympic bids and one of the largest sponsors of the Commonwealth Games.

Armed with a widely admired prospectus and the enthusiastic endorsement of Prime Minister John Major, Manchester took its £70 million 2000 Olympic bid to the 101st meeting of the IOC in Monte Carlo in September, 1993 with a sense of qualified optimism. The ten days of frantic final lobbying, receptions and parties in Monaco's plush hotels, attended by high-ranking government, business and entertainment figures from the five contending cities took on a surreal circus-like atmosphere.

At Manchester's star-studded garden party at the Beach Plaza Hotel, the movers and shakers hob-nobbed with, among other celebrity Brits, ex-Beatle Ringo Starr and diva Shirley Bassey.

"We could well have won," insisted Graham Stringer. "In the run up to Monte Carlo it was clearly possible. It was obvious that Sydney and Beijing were the two strongest cities, but the Chinese had human rights issues and Sydney was on the wrong side of the world. Bids from Adelaide and Melbourne had already failed and there was a perfectly reasonable analysis that says they did so because staging the games in Australia does not serve up live coverage for prime-time American television audiences, and TV rights are of crucial importance. On that basis, if it were to be Europe's turn, then Manchester had put forward a good bid with the full backing of the British government.

"We knew we had to get in front of Sydney and when you analyse the possibles and the maybes, that was possible - and then the Sydney votes would have come to us to stop Beijing."

According to Stringer, after John Major had breakfast with the Commonwealth delegates, they, led by Dick Pound, the Canadian vice president of the IOC who had toyed with the idea of supporting Beijing, decided that Sydney was ahead and that they would vote for the Australian bid.

With Brasilia, Milan and Tashkent having dropped out of the race before the final stage, there were five contenders with delegations crammed into the sweatbox of a concrete underground car park below Monaco's soccer pitch for the denouement at the "climax" of a tacky Eurovision-style variety show. The first round saw Istanbul despatched, having picked up seven votes to Berlin's nine, Manchester's eleven, Sydney's 30 and Beijing's 32. The

Chinese capital was further ahead of Sydney in the second round 37-30; Manchester scored fifteen and Berlin was eliminated with nine. Manchester was next to go out, the vote falling back to eleven, but when the total was split between the finalists it tipped the decision Sydney's way by 45-43 – the second narrowest margin in Olympic history.

When the news was broadcast live to crowds assembled in Manchester, the partying barely faltered. Though the bid was lost, the gains were substantial. Moreover the bid leaders were determined not to let the momentum slow; within weeks Graham Stringer and Bob Scott called a press conference to announce the city's bid for the Commonwealth Games in the Queen's Golden Jubilee year, 2002.

There were widespread misgivings. The Commonwealth Games, though billed as the biggest single multi-sports event ever staged in Britain, would attract far less in sponsorship and television rights than the Olympics, but once again, sport wasn't the real issue.

Stringer admitted: "It was a simple and straightforward decision all about the regeneration of east Manchester which had been stopped by the economic fall-out from Black Wednesday. In our view, by far the most powerful regenerative element of the Games was the stadium and we saw the Commonwealth Games as the way of securing it."

Howard Bernstein, at the time the city's deputy chief executive, and later knighted for services to the city, concurred. "I saw the Commonwealth Games bid very positively. We had our vision for east Manchester and if we were going to realise it in the quickest possible time, we had to find a mechanism for delivering a transformational development programme, and that was SportCity. Interestingly enough, while there were doubters, some of the people who criticised our Olympic bids were supportive of the Commonwealth Games initiative because its scale would be more manageable."

What isn't generally known is that the kind of Commonwealth Games that Manchester set off in pursuit of in 1993 wasn't the spectacle eventually staged in 2002. The XV Commonwealth Games in Canada in 1994 was relatively small-scale. Organisers "borrowed" the University of Victoria's Centennial Stadium for track and field events; there were 2,450 competitors from 63 nations in ten sports. The ante was upped considerably for Kuala Lumpur in 1998 by a showboating Malaysian government out to prove the success of its "Tiger economy" – witness the twin Petronas Towers, completed that year as the world's tallest building at 1,483ft. And by 2002 the scale and prestige of the Games would inflate still further.

Bernstein said: "We got locked into it. We were seeking a step up from Victoria, but not to the extent that Malaysia took it, which Manchester ended up having to promote and deliver. So the choice with which the government was presented over the Commonwealth Games was; now Manchester has won this for Britain, we need national support and we can either have the police band at the opening ceremony or something the nation can be proud of."

The revival of the 80,000-seat stadium proposals, still regarded as the key to regenerating east Manchester, would also put Manchester in contention to build a new national stadium to replace Wembley. The futuristic design that had drawn admiration from the International Olympic Committee was pitched against a swiftly cobbled-together plan from Wembley for the prize of more than £100 million of Lottery funding through Sport England, the former Sports Council. Though the Manchester and Wembley bids were short-listed, it quickly became apparent that the "competition" was a sham, not least when the Football Association, who were supposed to be assessing the contenders, took a controlling interest in Wembley. The "judge" had become a rival.

"The FA behaved like shits," Stringer said. "They were prejudiced from the start. They wanted to keep control of their fixture lists, FA Cup finals and semi-finals and England's internationals as a monopoly to use as a supply of freebies for themselves and their cronies. That's putting it at its most cynical but there's a significant base of the establishment ready to buy into that. It's the great untold story." Most accounts of what became a long drawn out national scandal over Wembley – the FA's reneging on the original requirement of a national stadium with a running track capable of hosting multi-sports events, its spiralling costs and failure to meet construction deadlines – begin in 1999. In fact this unsavoury saga began four years earlier and the way Manchester and sports fans throughout the country were cheated has been conveniently airbrushed from history.

Manchester thought long and hard about crying foul and challenging the decision to award the national stadium to Wembley But it would have meant not only fighting the FA and Sport England, but also the mind-set of the London-based media. To them it was unthinkable to have such a prestigious national facility anywhere outside the capital, no matter how inaccessible Wembley was for the rest of the country.

Clearly it had not been a fair competition, but at the same time that the Wembley decision was announced by Sport England, it was also revealed that Manchester would receive funding for its own stadium and for the aquatics centre, both key to the delivery of the Commonwealth Games. Taking the cash and then challenging the Wembley decision would have made Manchester appear ungrateful for the financial support it had received. Moreover, Stringer believed that the FA had made conciliatory noises about relaxing its monopoly of England fixtures.

"That was my interpretation and I remember making a speech in the council to that effect, but ten years later it's turned out to be completely wrong. They spread the fixtures about while Wembley was being redeveloped, but when it is completed we'll be back to the same monopolistic situation.

"We had thought of seeking a judicial review of the Wembley decision and we had very strong legal advice that the procurement of Wembley had been in breach of European competition law as well." Stringer contended that though the competition between Manchester and Wembley was a major contest for a public sector contract worth many tens of millions of pounds, it had not been advertised in the European Journal (OJEU) as required by law. The European legislation covers organisations and projects which receive public money, such as local authorities, NHS trusts, and central government departments. Some privately-funded managed contracts are also covered if projects are in receipt of more than 50 per cent of public funds – the Lowry arts centre in Salford and the Millennium Dome being cases in point. Around 2,500 notices are advertised every week, including invitations to tender, pre-information notices and contract award notices from throughout the EU and beyond.

The other twist in the saga involved the World Athletics Championships of 2003 which were to be staged in Paris, raising fears in London that a successful tournament would add weight to the French capital's anticipated bid for the 2012 Olympic Games. The then Secretary of State for Culture, Media and Sport, Chris Smith, had wanted the 2003 World Athletics Championships in London, but there was no chance of a venue being built in time. Stringer approached Smith and offered to stage the event in Manchester. The deal would have involved "buying" the championships from the International Amateur Athletics Federation (IAAF) – unlike the Olympics there is no bidding process for the World Championships - compensating Paris and building a larger stadium in Manchester, its capacity 58,000 instead of the 38,000 seats eventually built for the Commonwealth Games.

"There was a six week period during which we could have changed the footprint of what became the City of Manchester Stadium," Stringer revealed. "But Smith went round saying that the IAAF would only countenance the championships taking place in London, which was not true, and eventually talked our proposal out. There were some preliminary discussions with the IAAF in Paris, but we lost the deadline; the time frame closed. So Manchester was screwed twice over. We were first cheated out of building an 80,000-seat national stadium and then lost the chance to build one of 58,000 for the Commonwealth Games, which, when you think back, we could have filled. It would have meant that Manchester City FC would not take possession of their new stadium until a year later, but the club could have played at Maine Road for another twelve months. There was nothing fundamental to stop that.

"Had Manchester cried foul over Wembley, the only thing we could have done was to seek a judicial review and start proceedings in the European

Court to get Sport England and the FA to the negotiating table. You never know how these things might turn out, but it would have meant making enemies of the people who were baking the bread, so to speak. These are judgement calls. We may have got it completely wrong; maybe we should have played harder ball than we did, but what we did know was that in the end the government would have to put more money into the Commonwealth Games, which they did. If we'd decided to fight everybody, would we have got that money? These are all calculations you have to make. I'm not saying that we got everything right, but those were the issues at the time. I have no doubt we could have stopped Wembley for a long time through the legal process."

Nonetheless, the City of Manchester Stadium did become a reality in time for the Commonwealth Games in 2002 – scaled down to 38,000 seats, but rising to 48,000 when the running track was lifted prior to it becoming the new home of Manchester City Football Club for the 2003-04 season. Its cost was £110 million, of which Sport England provided £77 million, and it was delivered on time. By contrast, the bill for the new Wembley, still not completed ten years after "winning the competition", was more than £750 million. Pledges that Wembley could host the 2006 FA Cup Final were broken; it is doubtful whether Wembley would have been able to host the 2006 World Cup Finals even had they been awarded to England, but worst of all, when London stages the 2012 Olympic Games, Wembley will be sidelined. The London games will require yet another multi-million pound stadium and Wembley will host the finals of the Olympic soccer competition in which team Great Britain doesn't even take part because the English FA and their Scottish, Northern Irish and Welsh counterparts fear they would come under FIFA pressure to merge for future World Cup tournaments.

In the city centre too, a creative critical mass was taking shape. The down-at-heel textile district around the old Smithfield Market and once-bustling Oldham Street, commercially crippled by competition from the Arndale Centre, was branded The Northern Quarter and young entrepreneurs, attracted by cheap space for business and living, began to move in. One of the brightest was Tom Bloxham, founder of Urban Splash, whose vision kick-started the fashion for "loft living" in renovated properties and the concept, enthusiastically taken up by the council, of the 24-hour city. Across the city centre, the long-awaited redevelopment of the massive Victorian goods warehouse complex of the former Great Northern Railway was coming on stream. The new optimism, born from a "can-do" partnership approach to driving change was encapsulated in the City Pride Prospectus of 1994, drawing together more than 150 organisations and agencies.

But in an instant, as all the pieces of the developing city's vast jigsaw were falling neatly into place; as the sun shone on tens of thousands of Saturday morning shoppers mingling with football supporters from Italy, Germany, Russia and the Czech Republic, all in town for the Group D matches of the Euro '96 Championship, Manchester was faced with the most devastating calamity since the Second World War.

Chapter Twelve

Grand Designs

DEPUTY Prime Minister Michael Heseltine's arrival in a Manchester still struggling to come to terms with the catastrophe was eagerly anticipated.

On Wednesday 26th June, eleven days after the blast, the devastating scale of the damage and its potential impact on the city's future was sinking in and, despite all the initial bravado, the demand for the establishment of a task force headed by a minister of Cabinet rank to spearhead a £500 million rebuilding drive, spoke volumes about the crisis Manchester knew it was facing. The most urgent requirements were a clear declaration of support from the government to help restore confidence amongst the business community and immediate help for bombed-out small traders.

On emerging from talks with council leader Richard Leese and senior town hall officials, Heseltine savaged the bombers for "a barbaric act that cannot be sufficiently condemned" and praised the "extraordinary resilience" of the people of the city. He also pledged an immediate £50,000 donation for the Lord Mayor's Fund, set up to help small businesses relocate.

But what galvanised his audience the most was his commitment that the government would not only help Manchester reinstate the damage, but would also seize the opportunity to do much more. He declared that construction would be thrown open to an international competition seeking a range of ideas and imaginative concepts to take the city into the 21st Century.

On his train journey north, Heseltine had reflected on his past association with Manchester and how he knew it well, having first been involved with the redrawing of the city boundaries as a junior minister in the 1970s. Ten years later he had also played a critical role in the development of the redundant Central Railway Station into the G-Mex exhibition centre and in finding a way to finance the Bridgewater Hall, the new home of the Hallé Orchestra. There had been the City Challenge initiative in Hulme, too, and Heseltine's involvement with the failed 2000 Olympic bid, from which the Commonwealth Games was secured with a green light for the stadium, Velodrome and Aquatics Centre, which, he thought, was a significant legacy.

"As I remembered all this I resolved that what we needed was to turn disaster into opportunity", he wrote in his autobiography. "But how? This was a Labour council and unlikely to feel particularly at ease with a Conservative minister. I decided, however, to give it a go."

Heseltine's memoir was overly melodramatic; he need not have worried about his reception. In fact Manchester's attitude, despite the change of leadership only a few weeks before, remained the same. When it came to seeking the best way forward for the city, political ideology now came a distant second to pragmatic solutions. No sooner had he and Richard Leese got together, Heseltine recalled, that the council leader asked for the Deputy Prime Minister's views without offering his own.

"I told him I believed this was a remarkable opportunity to create a great legacy from the outrage," Heseltine said. "Rather than simply patching things up, I suggested they appoint – as a result of an international competition – the most imaginative urban landscape architects they could find, who should be invited to come up with ideas not just to rebuild the damaged streets, but a much wider area around the heart of Manchester." To be feasible, he insisted that the initiative would require a genuine public-private sector partnership; but Heseltine was pushing at an open door. Both he and the city had seen how this had worked in Hulme. Heseltine suggested that Sir Alan Cockshaw, chairman of AMEC, who had played a key role in City Challenge, be invited to lead the private sector team.

"I waited with apprehension for the objections. They did not come," Heseltine later revealed. "Instead Richard Leese said; 'I agree, that's what we will do'. It was a remarkable moment. I promised to give whatever support I properly could as a minister and undertook to keep closely in touch, both of which I did. We never had a disagreement and I was able to ensure that, one way or another, central government provided the financing on the scale necessary to complete the project."

Leese later described this pivotal moment in a slightly different way, suggesting that the city council's role was by no means as passive to the fount of ideas that Heseltine claimed as his own. "The support we got from Heseltine was phenomenal; on the first visit he gave me his home telephone number and invited me to call him any time, but we knew what we wanted," said the council leader.

Before Leese, Bernstein and David Trippier were invited to address Heseltine's meeting with key private sector figures, Trippier had asked: "What's the line?" Leese responded: "It's this: we want a masterplan to rebuild the city centre and take this as an opportunity." He later explained: "I think we'd already been able to sneak into Heseltine's script the idea of having an international design competition during prior discussions so we expected him to say it. He likes grand schemes so we gave him one. We sowed the seed of an idea in his mind that we thought he'd probably like."

The idea wasn't entirely new to Manchester. The city had been in competition with others to secure City Challenge funding for Hulme's regeneration. And in 1994 – two years ahead of the bomb - Manchester City Council had invited expressions of interest for an international design competition for the refurbishment and extension of the Manchester Art Gallery. That process attracted 132 architects and six teams were selected to proceed to the final design stage before Hopkins Architects were announced winners in January 1995. In neighbouring Salford, design competitions had been a regular feature in the development of the Quays in the city's former docklands.

Heseltine was aware of the immediate risks of implementing a longer-term reconstruction strategy as opposed to the fastest repair job possible, and on emerging from his meeting with Leese declared: "Our priority is getting Manchester back to work – but there is an opportunity, perhaps a unique opportunity, to rebuild a city for the 21ˢᵗ Century. There is an element of conflict between these two views, but there are ways of bridging them."

When he returned to Manchester exactly a week later to unveil an initial £21 million aid package top-sliced from European funds, Heseltine again spoke of the dilemma over a swift repair job or grander strategy facing the city. "I will be very surprised if hundreds of millions of pounds are not committed to the development of the city centre over the next few years," he said. "In three year's time no-one will doubt that the road we have chosen is the right one."

The temptation to repair and reinstate as quickly as possible was driven by the imminent opening of Britain's biggest out-of-town shopping mall just over five miles to the west, close to the banks of the Manchester Ship Canal at a village called Dumplington. The Trafford Centre – now a £650 million complex of 280 shops and stores, 38 restaurants, twenty cinema screens and 10,000 free car parking spaces - was the real prize at the heart of the ten-year-struggle for control of the Manchester Ship Canal Company. By the mid-1980s, the merchant shipping that had sailed the waterway's 35-mile length and made Manchester England's third biggest port had – like much of the industry it served – long gone.

The Trafford Centre had been first conceived by property tycoon John Whittaker's Peel Holdings in 1984 and formal plans were submitted in 1986. Soon afterwards Peel acquired a controlling interest in the site by winning its bitter share takeover battle for the canal; the goal was not the waterway and port, but the land and property that came with it.

The potential retail impact and other issues were debated for six long months at the Greater Manchester Retail Planning Inquiry in 1987 when nine out of the county's ten local authorities – Trafford was the lone supporter – stood in opposition, and eighteen months later a Department of the Environment press release finally declared "Chris Patten says Trafford Centre is best". It was far from the end of the story. Objectors – with

Manchester in the vanguard – mounted a lengthy and costly legal challenge that was not resolved until the House of Lords overturned a decision by the Court of Appeal and reinstated planning permission. Construction began on the 1.4 million square feet of retail space less than a month before the IRA blitzed Manchester.

It was apparent that when the Trafford Centre opened for business on September 10, 1998, much of Manchester city centre would still be closed off; in those circumstances, taking the longer view over reshaping the city was a brave decision. Even so, with the benefit of a decade of hindsight, some critics claimed that the remodelling plan was not radical enough. Sir Gerald Kaufman, Manchester's longest-serving MP – for Gorton, in east Manchester – chairman of the Commons Culture, Media and Sport select committee from 1997 to 2005, lamented to the Estates Gazette that development had been "reasonably good but not marvellous"; nothing to compare with Birmingham's Bull Ring and, even worse, it had been "a lost opportunity".

Manchester Civic Society contended that the redevelopment did not go nearly far enough in improving the city centre's historically woeful lack of open space. Manchester had plenty of parkland within the city boundaries, not least Wythenshawe Park and Heaton Park - one of the biggest municipally-owned parks in Europe - but they were on the on the southern and northern fringes respectively. Manchester's profit-hungry Victorians may have created the UK's first council-owned parks – Phillips Park in Beswick and Queen's Park in Harpurhey - but saw city centre parks as a waste of valuable land. Piccadilly Gardens only existed because the old Infirmary, which covered the site, had been demolished and rebuilt two miles further down Oxford Road. St Peter's Square and St John's Gardens are the sites of demolished churches and St Mary's Parsonage, a quiet quadrangle off Deansgate, hardly rates as a park.

Moreover, the Masterplan's original proposal for the creation of green space on the Salford side of the Irwell opposite Manchester Cathedral never materialised. But fears that the Trafford Centre could repeat Meadowhall's negative impact on Sheffield city centre – which fell from 9th to 23rd in the shopping league table - without the additional shattering effect of the biggest terrorist bomb detonated on the UK mainland – necessitated some degree of balance and compromise.

On July 4th, Heseltine again sought to rally the strategy's doubters. "There is a conflict between trying to get back into operation at the earliest possible moment or looking at the wider centre over a longer period of time. We think the latter is the route to recommend. There will be a whole range of difficult decisions, each with its own controversy, but in three years no-one will doubt that what has been decided is the right route to progress."

Two weeks after the bombing and resolved to turn catastrophe to opportunity, the task force charged with steering the regeneration of the city centre beyond its shattered core was assembled. It was like a reunion. Manchester Millennium Ltd, as suggested by Heseltine, appointed AMEC's Sir Alan Cockshaw as chairman, with council leader Richard Leese as deputy. Howard Bernstein, then deputy Chief Executive at the town hall and forging a formidable reputation as a fixer and a doer of exceptional vision, became MML's Chief Executive.

Bernstein recognised the moment as the most difficult facing his home city during his public-sector career, begun as a junior clerk at Manchester town hall in 1971. At that time Bernstein was the clear favourite amongst the candidates to be appointed Chief Executive of English Partnerships, the national regeneration agency, but in the wake of the disaster that had overtaken the city, he decided to stay in Manchester. When Cockshaw was invited to chair the task force, his response was that he would accept if Bernstein, who had the confidence of both the city and the private sector, became its Chief Executive.

"I couldn't turn it down; this was my city," he said. "The city centre, both before and after the bomb, was challenging for me for different reasons. Firstly, failure to succeed would mean a real downturn in the city's fortunes. Secondly, there was an acute sense that people's livelihoods had been affected and we had to assist in their relocation, especially because at that

The Ford Cargo van packed with explosives

Detonation!

The shattered walkway between the Arndale Centre and Marks and Spencer's

Inside the shattered bridge - a picture never before published

An aerial view of the devastation

An engine block from the Ford Cargo van lying amongst office debris

The ruined escalator in the Arndale Centre

Shops were torn apart

People mistook fallen mannequins for corpses

A city in shreds

The lone survivor at ground zero

New Cathedral Street with the mediaeval Shambles in the distance

The new bridge with the Urbis building towering behind

same time we were facing the opening of the Trafford Centre which would have been bad enough had we been firing on all cylinders, but became especially so when we'd just lost more than a quarter of our retail space. Thirdly, there were challenges we set ourselves with the interdependence of the public and private sector investments that were critical to the delivery of every element of the development."

MML's other board members were Sir David Trippier who ten years earlier, as Inner Cities' Minister, had invited a former left-wing city council leader to join the pioneering Central Manchester Urban Development Corporation; Marianne Neville-Rolfe, director, Government Office North West and as such, the region's most senior civil servant; Tony Strachan, agent for the Bank of England; Kath Robinson, deputy leader of the city council and "councillor for fun", Pat Karney, chair of the city centre sub-committee.

The tightly structured team, who knew each other well, seconded staff from the town hall, accountants KPMG, Natwest Bank, GONW and others and took up residence in Fountain Street with a formidable mission before them.

Trippier, the former Tory minister, who acknowledged that his appointment as chairman of the newly formed, Manchester Airport-funded promotional organisation, Marketing Manchester, wouldn't have happened without Graham Stringer's influence (Stringer was still chairman of the airport), said: "For me the reaction to the bomb blast was of immense significance. Those of us who knew Manchester well had not the slightest doubt in our minds that we could turn what appeared to be a tragedy into a glorious opportunity. Once again the confidence of the people living in the area shone through. I am not entirely certain that had the bomb gone off ten years earlier, the same degree of confidence would have been in evidence."

The Task Force lost no time in setting the wheels in motion. The international design competition for a master-plan for the regeneration of the city centre, taking in not only the bomb-blasted areas, but also incorporating the historic area around Manchester Cathedral, was launched on July 17th with a deadline for expressions of interest set for August 23rd and a date for the announcement of the winner put at November 5th.

The Task Force's first priority, according to Bernstein, was to make sure the city became operational again as efficiently as it could in the shortest possible time. That meant striving to relocate bombed out businesses large and small – from Marks & Spencer, then the biggest retailer in Britain, to the tarot card readers and postcard stalls of the Corn Exchange's flea market. Initial progress seemed remarkable. It was only two weeks after the bombing that the market traders became operational at the High Street end of the Arndale Centre, the furthest point in the mall from the worst of the blast damage. The occasion was marked with what was to become the usual Mancunian flourish, a carnival atmosphere, the presence of the Lord Mayor and an afternoon of karaoke in Piccadilly.

By July 10th the temporary home of Marks & Spencer had also been identified – 90,000 square feet of space on the upper floors of the Lewis's department store on the corner of Market Street and Piccadilly, negotiated by its then owner, the retail tycoon Philip Green, and premises in Spring Gardens to accommodate the all-important food hall. Their official opening drew thousands of shoppers determined to make a point and a reciprocal show of loyalty. Marks & Spencer's chairman was guest of honour and Alex Ferguson, manager of Manchester United, and Steve Coppell, fleetingly manager of Manchester City, put in celebrity appearances. The top floor of the Lewis's location also provided a home for 22 businesses bombed out of the Royal Exchange shopping centre. Elsewhere, however, the small traders' plight had become critical and there was rising concern that little financial help was on the way from central government.

Baroness Dean of Thornton-le-Fylde – Brenda Dean, the Manchester-born former print union boss – told the House of Lords on July 24: "Manchester needs help to help itself in this situation. This is a national issue, not a city issue or concerned with one small geographical area. I suggest in perhaps the gentlest way that the help that Manchester needs has not been recognised by the Government. That help is needed especially by small traders. Of course, visits by the Deputy Prime Minister are very welcome indeed. I applaud those visits. But the gloss soon disappears and the people of Manchester realise that the wonderful announcement of £20 million in support that has been found for them is, in fact, merely relocated money. I gather that it is not new money but comes from the European Fund allocation for the area of Greater Manchester, Cheshire and Lancashire over the 1996-97 period."

Dean paid tribute to the big retailers like Marks & Spencer and Mothercare, who had responded to the crisis so positively, but stressed that it was the small firms that were most vulnerable. Many did have insurance and had been told that the government-funded terror attack compensation scheme that recompensed bombed-out businesses in Northern Ireland was not appropriate on the UK mainland. In England insurance against terrorist attack was available for those prepared to pay for it; in Northern Ireland, a battle zone for almost three decades, there was no such insurance cover.

She spelled out the small traders' "impossible situation." They were too small, crammed together and could not get at their stock to replenish and start up as new businesses. "We are heading for what would have been a very busy period for them in the lead-up to Christmas. What are they going to do? They face genuine hardship with relocation costs; creditors need paying. What do these businesses have to help them in Manchester? They have the Lord Mayor's Emergency Fund."

Two days after Dean made her Westminster plea, more than 100 bombed-out traders from the Corn Exchange staged a protest demonstration over being denied access to their stock six weeks after the blast. The building's owners claimed it was too dangerous. It was another five weeks before the first seventeen of them were able to re-open for business in a new location, a building in Church Street in the Northern Quarter grandly named The Coliseum.

By the first anniversary of the attack, many of the key decisions that set the city on the road to recovery had been taken and the defiant statement that Manchester would be back, better than ever, was just beginning to be realised. The ecumenical service at Manchester Cathedral on Sunday, 15th June, 1997, timed at exactly the moment the bomb had exploded twelve months earlier, provided a moment of stocktaking and reflection.

The Very Rev Ken Riley, then Dean, welcomed a congregation of more than 2,000, including representatives of all sections of the community, by recalling that many of those gathered in the cathedral that morning had come with their own emotions, thoughts and prayers as they remembered that dreadful day. Some had narrowly escaped death, many had been injured; others lost their homes or their livelihoods and everyone had been stunned by the sheer scale of the damage.

His words on that day resounded through the following decade. "There is a saying that God sometimes allows us magnificent opportunities, brilliantly disguised as insoluble problems, and that has been something of Manchester's experience over the past year, as we have tried to play our part in the age-old human story of the constant struggle to keep hope alive, to bring good out of evil and new life out of the ashes of destruction."

The story of the city's reaction to disaster unfolded as the service proceeded, reflecting first on the events of that sunny day in June 1996, then finding that shining through the noise, confusion and devastation had been the bravery and devotion to duty of the police, firefighters and ambulance crews and with them, the surgeons, doctors and nurses who were being honoured. Thanks were also due, he said, for all that had been achieved in getting much of Manchester back to business through the Lord Mayor's Appeal Fund and the staff in the town hall who had "worked so tirelessly not only in helping individuals but also in directing the restoration of the city.

"Finally," said Riley, "we look forward to the renewal of the city, 'fair as she might be', and pray that the rebuilding of physical structures may go hand in hand with the rebuilding and strengthening of the community – as T S Eliot reminds us: 'We build in vain unless the Lord build with us'."

Chapter Thirteen

Masterplan

THE notion that the biggest bomb ever detonated on the UK mainland in peacetime was the best thing that ever happened to Manchester or, a blessing in disguise, is frequently voiced. The sentiment that it was a pity the explosion didn't happen closer to Piccadilly Plaza demonstrates that Mancunians are still not comfortable with their modernist architecture of the 1960s and 1970s, though the refurbishment of the hotel, office and retail complex overlooking the remodelled Piccadilly Gardens – which have also drawn criticism – may alter the less jaundiced view.

Richard Leese, leader of Manchester city council and Sir Howard Bernstein, the town hall's chief executive, however, dismiss the "blessing" argument out of hand. Firstly the IRA wounded more than 200 people, mercifully only a handful seriously, and inflicted disruption and hardship upon many more. And for all the magnificent response of the authorities in the aftermath of the bomb, businesses did close and people did lose their jobs. Further, the argument that the bomb changed everything in Manchester is far from the truth. On the contrary, had everything not already changed in Manchester – certainly from the political perspective – from the revolutionary days of the mid-1980s, it is quite feasible that the city could not have recovered and prospered in the way that it has.

As Sir David Trippier, the former Inner Cities Minister, first chief of Marketing Manchester and member of the rebuilding task force asserted: "The bomb went off in a city that had become confident with itself. People said this is a problem we will sort. No-one had the slightest doubt that the city centre would come back better than before. But if that bomb had gone off before 1987 I don't know what would have happened. At that time morale was on the floor; no-one could see their way out of any of the problems."

Graham Stringer, who became Labour MP for Blackley after leading the city council for a dozen years, made the same point, though in a slightly different way. "If you had to have a bomb go off in the middle of a thirteen year period, then 1996 was probably the best time. All the partnerships that responded to the situation had been tried and tested, the Trafford Centre was not yet open and the Commonwealth Games was still six years away."

Ten years on, both Bernstein and Leese claim that most of the much-praised changes in the city centre that were accomplished in the wake of the blast would have been achieved anyway. Before the explosion Bernstein had already been in talks with the key landowners, Marks & Spencer, P&O, then owners of the Arndale Centre, and the Prudential, owners of the Royal Exchange. Frogmore Estates, having only taken over the Corn Exchange shortly before June 15th, had been outside the loop until after the blast. Speaking as the tenth anniversary of the explosion approached, he said: "We all knew what we wanted to do; we knew that the core of the city centre was dysfunctional and the historic area around the Cathedral and Chetham's was cut off. There was a requirement to re-plan and the catastrophe of the bomb just gave us the opportunity to accelerate that process which otherwise might have taken ten years. In fact it took us just three of four, but it would have been done now, more or less, in my opinion."

Marks & Spencer's was looking to expand its site and had been in talks with the Royal Insurance Company in next-door Longridge House which was in what is now Exchange Square. But the real key to unlocking redevelopment was identified as the Safeway supermarket leaving the Market Place precinct, freeing up that space, which, according to Bernstein, was just a matter of time. Leese took a similar line. "I don't think it's true that the bomb was the major turning point because by 1996, Manchester was already on an agenda for change. While the blast provided a specific opportunity to re-plan and reconstruct a particular part of the city centre, much of the process of change was already under way."

Another task force member, Pat Karney, is also reluctant to accept the contention that the bomb was good for the city. Ten years on he still experiences anxieties thinking about what might have happened.

"It wasn't a good thing for Manchester," he insisted. "That idea was constantly put to us, but I saw the woman who worked in the insurance building who suffered the facial injuries. I still shudder, not least because I was in fear for my own life and the lives of members of my family. So the first reference point always has to be the human cost. The changes brought about in the city have been tremendous – I still remember my first sight of the computer-generated view along New Cathedral Street from St Ann's to the Cathedral and it was joyous. But I do think that in the last ten years that every city in Britain has grown and reinvented itself. So the bomb wasn't some great saviour. That was a period when cities rediscovered themselves and people fell in love with them and wanted to live in city centres. It's happened in Birmingham, Newcastle and Leeds as well and the evidence is there in terms of population."

It was possible, in the wake of the bomb, that the reconstruction programme benefited from a slightly higher commitment of central government funding, but it has to be borne in mind that, given the totality of the investment in the new city centre, Whitehall's contribution was relatively small. By 1996 Manchester had been named host city for the 2002 Commonwealth Games and arguably that nomination – and the facilities developed to support the earlier Olympic bids – had more of an impact on the city than the bombers.

Residential development was already well underway by 1996 with the development by Tom Bloxham's Urban Splash of Sally's Yard and Smithfield Buildings in the Northern Quarter and the conversion into apartments of former warehouses in Whitworth Street, all precursors of the boom to come.

At the time of the bomb blast, Sir Michael Hopkins' £35 million National Lottery-funded extension to Manchester Art Gallery had been given the go-ahead as had major additions to the Manchester Museum at the University in Oxford Road and the Museum of Science and Industry, and the construction of the Manchester Arena was progressing. Maxwell House, the old *Daily Mirror* printing plant in Withy Grove was also being looked at. The Co-operative Wholesale Society, headquartered in the next few blocks along Corporation Street had at one time been eyeing the site for redevelopment into a shopping centre; the massive entertainment complex that eventually went into the newspaper printworks might have opened instead within Piccadilly Plaza.

"A lot of things that changed the face of the city had either happened already, were happening or would have happened anyway," Leese asserted. "That was nothing to do with one physical event – the exploding of the IRA's bomb – but because the people and the learning were already in place. That's why we were able to respond to the bomb the way we did. The expertise would have been applied to the city without the bomb, though obviously in different circumstances."

Whatever the merits of Leese's case, most Mancunians who compared the devastation of 1996 to the city centre ten years on would say his logic was coloured by 20x20 hindsight and fraught with might-have-beens. The counter view, set out in a paper written by Salford University sociologists John Myles and Ian Taylor, reflected an underlying gloom. They claimed that anxieties associated with the looming opening of the Trafford Centre on the medium term viability of a refurbished Manchester city centre still pivoting around the unloved Arndale were not simply confined to the owners and tenants of the Arndale itself, but to many other key players in planning and local government circles.

Despite significant progress being made in encouraging people to take up residence in the city centre core, there was also continuing evidence in Manchester, as in many other cities, that many offices and businesses, as well as private citizens, were moving in the opposite direction. "The redesign of the city centre was taking place at a time when many commentators on the condition of cities were actually concerned as to the medium term viability of the idea of a city centre as such," they argued.

As it was, the unveiling of the five short-listed contenders for the city centre Masterplan competition – whittled down from 27 outline bids – attracted intense interest. Manchester Millennium Limited had asked for models and large exhibition boards of the proposals which would help people better appreciate what the concepts were about than reams of architectural drawings. When they went on display in the town hall, the place was, in the words of one task force member, "mobbed out".

The winner of the international design competition, announced with great ceremony on Guy Fawkes Day, November 5, 1996, was a consortium comprising the American urban design corporation EDAW; Manchester-based Ian Simpson Architects; Benoy BDP retail developers; transportation engineers Alan Baxter Associates and Johnson Urban Development Consultants.

Of all the members of the consortium, it was Ian Simpson who was the pivotal figure and, in the years that have followed, made the biggest impact on the cityscape, a dramatic process that will continue to unfold for the next ten years and beyond. It all began with a sketched idea on a scrap of paper that became the driving force behind the whole of the winning competitive bid and ultimately, the re-planning of the city centre. Simpson, born in Heywood, a mill town ten miles north of Manchester between Bury and Rochdale, regarded Manchester as his home city and knew it well from being a youngster and taking the bus into "town". After working in London he set up his practice with Rachel Haugh in the mid-1980s and by the early 1990s was involved in several small-scale architectural projects across the city, primarily awkward tasks involving listed buildings.

They produced the original master plan for the Knott Mill area of the city which developed loft apartments and office space for creative businesses in a warren of old industrial premises on the edge of the city centre, and had worked with Jim Ramsbottom, the bookie-turned-developer in Castlefield. The centrepiece project was the refurbishment into high-tech business space of Merchant's Warehouse, a derelict semi-ruin dating from the late 18th Century on the long-disused quayside of James Brindley's pioneering

Bridgewater Canal. When the bomb exploded, Ian Simpson Architects were also working on the extension of the Manchester Museum, housed within Manchester University's 19th Century Owens College in Oxford Road.

Like many people who travelled into Manchester from north of the city, but with his architect's eye, Simpson was acutely aware of the north-south divide in microcosm; the massive blast presented him with the opportunity to do something about it. The Masterplan competition was a two stage bid process. From the outset, Simpson gathered a team of architects and invited EDAW, who had been involved in several other projects in the city, to come on board. Simpson recalled: "With that we also had Alan Baxter and Associates as structural engineers and Benoy, giving us some advice on retail. But we actually did the first phase independently of EDAW; it was only the second stage, when the bidders were short-listed to five teams, that EDAW actually engaged with the process.

"In the first place we set out our ambition with a sketch I did originally designed to break that north-south barrier with a physical and visual extension of St Ann's Square which ultimately became New Cathedral Street. It was a simple, perpendicular line bisecting St Mary's Gate, cutting across in line with St Ann's Square. In fact, prior to the design competition, the BBC on a Newsnight programme asked four designers for their ideas of what they would do if they were given the chance and I came up with this before and after. It was the idea I had right from the outset which was the driving force of the whole of the bid, really.

"To the north of the divide, the Corn Exchange was full of tat. The Printworks was derelict and the site of Urbis was a car park. There were all those offices around the Market Place development that couldn't be let for £6 per square foot. There was very little value beyond the old Marks & Spencer store; the city sort of stopped there. But to the south, there was King Street and Kendal's and I just thought – as an idea – to spread the value from south to north you needed a physical and visual means of linking the old Mediaeval quarter around the Cathedral, which was a great asset, to the rest of the city."

Simpson's Masterplan for transforming Manchester into "the finest city centre in Europe" was inherently that simple. The key elements were to reconnect previously isolated areas of the city and give priority to pedestrians through the creation of active streets, squares and gardens and a vibrant centre that would appeal to people day and night. It was not intended to be a blueprint for development, as many people had imagined, but a flexible framework to inform and guide development, public and private, in the reconstruction of the bombed-out core and beyond. This provoked some misunderstanding, for it appeared to some commentators that the task force had chosen the "least ambitious" of the five options. Sir Alan Cockshaw, the task force chairman commended the Masterplan's simplicity and countered that it was, in fact, a very radical proposal, adding that the memorable city centre that would rise from the rubble represented "a remarkable demonstration of the futility of terrorism". The vision would create a city fit for the 21st Century, but more importantly, one that Mancunians could be proud of.

Unattractive Market Place was demolished to accommodate New Cathedral Street

Before the bomb, Manchester's retail core had suffered from the impact of dysfunctional 1960s and 1970s development exacerbated by the impact of traffic growth. Immediately to the north, the Mediaeval heart of the city, which had taken shape around the Cathedral site on an elevated bluff above the confluence of the rivers Irwell and Irk – the latter now gushes from the culvert taking it beneath Victoria railway station – were cut off from the rest of the city. A combination of busy roads, awkward changes in level and the blank urban walls of the Arndale Centre and dismal Market Place made the pedestrian route, if not quite completely impenetrable, then very unattractive. The main road, Corporation Street, was busy with traffic and dominated by the blank yellow-tiled wall of the Arndale.

All this was to change. Condemning Market Place to be swept from the map would enable the creation of a completely new, pedestrian boulevard – New Cathedral Street - and dramatic changes to the Corporation Street façade of the Arndale plus a significant restriction of traffic, would enable the rediscovery of another user-friendly route.

It really was that simple. Pedestrians would be able to wander between St Ann's Church and the Cathedral with views between the two uninterrupted for the first time in more than a century. The city centre would be stretched northwards to include Shudehill and Cannon Street, the fume-filled concrete canyon between the two megalithic blocks of the Arndale Centre, which had served as a makeshift, down-at-heel bus station, was earmarked as a winter garden beneath a new glass atrium. Manchester's paucity of open space would be augmented by the creation of two new public squares, Exchange Square and Cathedral Gardens, and the redundant former newspaper production plant would be transformed into a 24-hour entertainment centre with restaurants, cinemas and bars.

Ten years on, Richard Leese dismissed charges that the Masterplan wasn't radical enough. What came out, he insisted, was a balanced scheme, but certainly not a compromise, despite the huge competitive threat from the opening of the Trafford Centre, two years away. The Masterplan was not an architectural exercise with detailed pictures of proposed new buildings

– those came later – it was a process.

"If we were going to make Manchester city centre work better, we had to ask ourselves what was wrong with it in the first place; what did we need to change? So we had to have a plan that addressed those issues. Secondly, it had to be deliverable. One of the rival proposals effectively said that the Arndale would have to come down – well, that was never going to happen. A city centre is, in essence a marketplace which has to work commercially, ultimately without subsidy and stand on its own feet. We wanted a plan that combined good planning principles and addressed the key issues like joining together modern and Mediaeval Manchester, and the EDAW proposals did that. When it came to delivering particular elements of the Masterplan, that's when we started getting the excitement and, in some cases, taking risks."

Risks? Leese cited the example of the futuristic footbridge across Corporation Street at first floor level between the Arndale Centre and Marks & Spencer's store, replacing the previous span that was destroyed when the Ford Cargo exploded beneath it. Neither the city council nor the task force wanted to replace the bridge at all and it was not included in the original Masterplan. But the commercial land leaseholders took the opposite view; they wanted to ensure the Arndale Centre was linked directly to the new Marks & Spencer store. After much debate, the city decided on compromise, providing it was a high quality bridge - and in doing so acquired a key bargaining counter enabling the acquisition of the old Shambles area from the head leaseholder.

"It was," conceded Sir Howard Bernstein, "a pricey bridge." He wasn't kidding: at £650,000, Hodder Associates' striking computer-generated steel and glass hyperbolic paraboloid structure turned out to be, measure for measure – it is only 62 feet long - one of the most expensive bridges the world has ever seen.

But in return Bernstein was able to buy the lease on the old Shambles in Market Place, an absolutely vital piece of the reconstruction jigsaw, for it was through here that New Cathedral Street, the most important element in the entire Masterplan, was to be driven.

The task force had worked closely with P&O, the head leaseholder of both the Arndale Centre and Market Place; nonetheless, P&O's sale of the properties to Prudential for £325 million, announced on 22nd December 1997, was a welcome development. "P&O were very good and had played a very fair game in developing the planning framework in those critical months," said Bernstein. "But when it became clear that P&O themselves would need to invest significant sums in the remodelled Arndale, they got out. It was important to us because we didn't believe that P&O ultimately had the investment appetite to drive the Arndale forward as we wanted and I think that judgement was well borne out when they sold to the Pru."

Bernstein also revealed that there had been a view at the time that Voyagers Bridge, spanning the mouth of Market Street between the Arndale and Boots' store should be demolished, but the idea was not progressed because it would have cost "an enormous sum of money that could not be justified." One bridge was removed, however, the span across Deansgate that cut across views of the Cathedral; declared redundant with the bulldozing of old Market Place.

Of the Corporation Street bridge, Leese said: "It was definitely an engineering challenge. The apertures in the two buildings are not at the same height, they don't face each other directly and they are not parallel." At more than £10,000 per twelve inches, little wonder the bridge was afforded the lofty status by the Royal Institute of British Architects of being "a symbol of Manchester's recovery from the bomb; a cutting edge symbol of modernity which captures the optimism of the city's growth and future."

Ironically, however, it was the Post Office's 100-year-old red pillar box, returned to its place just below the bridge by Royal Mail, that most Mancunians instead adopted as their symbol of recovery. The box survived the bomb almost intact and was taken to be repaired at Altrincham by the postman who was allowed across the police cordon to empty it several days after the blast. Chris Morris took personal charge of its future. "I'm a bit of an anorak about pillar boxes," he admitted. It now bears a plaque commemorating its survival.

Leese had been confident that if the city secured a good Masterplan, the exciting elements could be slotted neatly into it: the new Marks & Spencer's store, the remodelled Arndale built outwards into Corporation Street, Exchange Square, Cathedral Gardens, Ian Simpson's dazzling apartment and penthouse block at One Deansgate and what was to become Manchester's Millennium project, the still controversial "museum of modern life", Urbis. Yet in all of this the council leader saw the most radical element of the plan as what, superficially at least, seemed the least exciting; the creation of New Cathedral Street.

"It completely re-orientated the city," he said, "and the point that I knew that it worked was when I stood at the top of the steps to Exchange Square and could see the Cathedral and the relocated Shambles pubs in one direction and St Ann's Church in the other. That was the absolutely fundamental improvement and the winner was the only Masterplan to include it."

So does Ian Simpson, whose original and simple sketched vision attracted such acclaim, now share the notion that the transformation of Manchester would have happened whether the bombers had stuck or not?

"I am not sure," he said. "Even after the bomb and the acceptance by the Task Force of the Masterplan containing the idea of New Cathedral Street, it still took two years to get the landowners, P&O and Prudential, to agree there was any value in doing that. One of the reasons we won the argument was that it was an inherently simple strategy, one that the landowners, primarily based in London, could understand and see that it would actually be delivered. But it took a lot of time and effort on behalf of Manchester Millennium to convince them the merits of demolishing the Market Place precinct and punching a new thoroughfare through. We couldn't do anything without them; though the city council owned the freehold they had to get the people with the long leaseholds on the land to agree with us. They had their own designers and appraisers and there was a lot of sucking through teeth in terms of, 'Ooh, we're not sure'."

In fact the task force had more at its disposal during the protracted talks than friendly persuasion. A month after the winning Masterplan emerged, Manchester Millennium's negotiators armed themselves with a big stick – the anodyne-sounding Supplementary Planning Guidance Document. Its provisions effectively vetoed any notion that P&O and the Prudential may have harboured about picking up the insurance money and rebuilding what was there before the blast. Quite simply they would not have received planning permission to do so.

Simpson raised another major doubt as to whether Manchester city centre could have regenerated so successfully without the IRA's attack through the timing of Marks & Spencer's early commitment to building the company's biggest store, incorporating some of the site of the demolished insurance building next door. "It was a massive risk that did not really work for them," Simpson asserted. "Or they would not have later sold half the store to Selfridges."

He was making the point that while it may have been the slings and arrows aimed by the print media's fashionistas that caused the commercial ills that M&S was to suffer soon afterwards, rather than the millions invested in Manchester, had the events of June 15th 1996 not taken place, the huge investment pledged by the retailer, widely acknowledged as pivotal to the city centre's renewal, would surely have been open to question.

Though Sir Richard Greenbury had been true to his word, when the British Design Partnership and Bovis delivered the flagship store - almost a quarter of a million square feet on six levels – Marks & Spencer's fortunes were in such decline that less than two years after opening in November 1999, the company announced that Selfridges would take over half the floor space at the Exchange Square end of the building. If M&S faltered, Manchester city centre certainly did not.

When Selfridges opened their half of the building in September 2002 – they already operated one of the anchor stores in the Trafford Centre – it was proof that the city centre had not merely weathered the challenge from the massive out-of-town mall, but had the UK's top retailers clamouring for a piece of the action.

New Cathedral Street is now one of Manchester's most popular and attractive shopping avenues, the home of blue chip high street retailers including Harvey Nichols, Zara, Heals and L K Bennett. It is difficult to imagine Manchester without it.

Ian Simpson, architect of the 'Masterplan'

Chapter Fourteen

Back to the Future

THE Victorians had little time for sentiment amid their wealth and empire building exploits and as Manchester grew at an astonishing pace between the end of the 18th Century and the end of the 19th, the city's Mediaeval past was almost obliterated.

The Roman occupation began around AD70. It was little more than a garrisoned fortress built by General Julius Agricola at a defensible position against the local Celtic tribe, the Brigantes, on a low sandstone bluff above the confluence of the Irwell and Medlock. The original wooden fort, on the major road from Chester to York, covered five acres and was surrounded by woodland populated by wild boar and deer. Agricola named the spot Mamucium, literally "a breast-shaped hill", which was ironically in what is now Salford. There, the site is marked by Camp Street; Manchester appropriated the name. The later construction of a stone fort in what is now Castlefield must have come as something of a relief to the legionnaires posted to this damp, cold outpost from the Roman Empire's central European provinces and, over time, a small settlement grew around it. At its height some 2,000 people would have lived within its walls, including soldiers' families, local traders and craftsmen. But when the Romans abandoned it in 411, most traces of the settlement disappeared.

The village that reappeared as Anglo Saxon-Danish Mamecaestre some 500 years later was a mile upstream where the Irk joins the Irwell. The transition from hamlet to town started in the 13th Century and the establishment of the Mediaeval borough followed the foundation of the College of Priests at the local church in 1421. It lagged almost 200 years behind the granting of neighbouring Salford's charter by Ranulf, Earl of Cheshire in 1230, as Salfordians never tire of repeating. During the reign of Edward the Confessor in the 11th Century, Manchester was part of the Royal Manor of Salford.

Part of the original college survives within Chetham's School and the status of the church, later to become Manchester Cathedral, was enhanced accordingly.

Though Manchester became a relatively important cloth town, the population in 1772 was still only 25,000. The onset of the Industrial Revolution, however, saw the number swell to half a million in little over a century and to 700,000 by 1910. Aside from the cluster of old buildings around the Cathedral and the Old Shambles off St Mary's Gate, the rest was buried beneath the mills and warehouses of the Victorian city. Neither was heritage at the forefront of the minds of developers in the 1960s and 1970s.

The 1996 bomb, however, provided the opportunity to go back to the future: the Masterplan's Millennium Quarter.

Manchester Cathedral is no York Minster, nor does it have the setting of an Exeter, Wells or Salisbury in their delightful closes. It does, however, claim descent from a Saxon church on the site following the discovery of the Angel Stone, embedded in the wall of the original south porch, dated to around 700AD. The current church was begun in 1215 by Robert Greslet, 5th Baron of Manchester next to his manor house, now Chetham's Library, but much of the current building post-dates its elevation to Cathedral status in 1847. The new tower, an exact replica apart from being six feet higher than its predecessor, was opened in 1868; between 1882 and 1883 the whole of the nave interior was replaced, stone by stone, and six years later a new north porch was built followed by the south porch in 1891. Said to be the widest cathedral in the UK, Manchester also boasts some of the finest Mediaeval wood carving in the country. Such attractions, however, remained largely unseen by most modern Mancunians for, unlike many other cities, Manchester Cathedral was on the periphery of the city centre rather than a focal point. Moreover, the surrounding buildings that enclosed it looked away from the church instead of facing it.

With New Cathedral Street in place, the Masterplan ensured that the great church is once again in its rightful place in the heart of the city with, for the first time, a Visitor Centre in Cateaton Street. The new centre itself contains a fascinating glimpse into Manchester's Mediaeval past, unseen for centuries. The Hanging Bridge, an ancient monument built across the Hanging Ditch in 1421 to connect Manchester with its church, can be viewed and indeed touched in the centre's pleasant basement refectory.

Adjacent to the Cathedral and also benefiting from the Master-plan's success in opening up Manchester's heritage, is Chetham's School of Music which incorporates a historic library, together the most complete late-Mediaeval residential complex to survive in the north west of England. The buildings date from the second quarter of the 15th Century. The survival of so complete a set of Mediaeval buildings is rare and the troubled history of the buildings makes this survival all the more surprising.

In 1547 the College was dissolved under the Chantries Act and the buildings were purchased by the Earl of Derby who converted the property into a town residence. The College was re-founded as a Catholic foundation by Queen Mary, only to be closed down again on the accession of Elizabeth I. In 1578 it was formally established with a new charter as Christ's College and an arrangement was made with the Earl of Derby to allow the Warden and Fellows to re-occupy the College buildings.

Up to the Civil War the buildings remained in the hands of the Stanleys, Earls of Derby. Their fortunes had been made by the defection of Lord Stanley and his brother, Sir William, from the Yorkist King Richard III to Henry Tudor – later Henry VII – during the decisive last battle of the Wars of the Roses at Bosworth in 1485, and numerous signs of their ownership are still evident. During the War the buildings were used as a prison and arsenal, parts were allowed to become derelict, and the property was eventually taken over by the Parliamentary Committee of Sequestration.

It was then that Humphrey Chetham, a prosperous Manchester merchant, made his first overtures to purchase the College to house a school and library. Chetham died in 1653 before the negotiations were completed and it was left to his executors to carry out his intentions. His will stated that the bulk of his fortune was to be used to endow a hospital for the maintenance and education of 40 poor boys and to adapt and equip part of the building as a library for scholars. Chetham's Library continues to serve its founder's purpose, although the hospital has modified its activities through the centuries, eventually being re-established as a co-educational music school in 1969.

The Millennium Quarter also provides the latest, and probably last, home for the city's Old Shambles pubs, The Old Wellington and Sinclair's Oyster Bar. Elevated fifteen feet in the 1970s to make way for below-ground service roads to the then new Marks & Spencer's store, they survived the 1996 bombing but were directly in the path of the planned New Cathedral Street. The solution was even more drastic than the last one. This time the two ancient buildings were dismantled, piece by piece with every brick, tile, timber and slate carefully labelled and stored, then reassembled 400 yards away close to the Cathedral. Because the two adjoining in-line pubs would not fit in the gap between the Corn Exchange and the Mitre Hotel, they were reconstructed at right angles to each other with a modern stone building, designed in consultation with English Heritage, providing a "knuckle" link at the join. The reconfiguration did not suit some purists, but the new location was a masterstroke and the pubs look far more in tune with their surroundings than they had in the bleak concrete precinct. Both buildings have once again become freestanding rather than being spread-eagled against the concrete mass of the Market Place, enabling the rear of the Old Wellington to be restored to its original half-timbered form following considerable on-site research, while the rear elevation of Sinclair's was designed to reflect its essential character.

The scheme, for all its innovation and complexity, however, was far from universally praised. A lobby group styling itself SOS – Save Our Shambles – sponsored by the Manchester Civic Society, launched a campaign of opposition to the proposal to remove the pubs from their Market Place site. They argued that their earlier elevation had not been a "move" because the Shambles had to all intents and purposed remained on, or only slightly above, the spot where they were built. So vociferous was SOS's opposition that they likened the Masterplanners' decision to remove them as "an aftershock far more terrible in its destructive impact than the original bomb". The campaign leaflet added: "We don't want to demolish the Shambles to replicate a street in Barcelona or Turin." Their counter proposal was tantamount to recreating the pre-1970s street pattern that had been concreted over for the Market Place precinct. In the light of the massive commercial and political forces now at work, it was a rather quaint hope.

Masterplanner Ian Simpson was in no doubt that the pubs would have to move. "It was one of the big decisions we had to make and I was adamant that there was no way that we could plan around them. We had to get a line of sight from St Ann's to the Cathedral and it just so happened that it went straight through the middle of the Old Wellington Inn. I personally spent a lot of time convincing the pub owners and their architects that if they moved they would have a much better location. But it was like, 'Ooh, we're not sure about being stuck at the end of New Cathedral Street, we're going to lose trade.' But just compare where they are now with where they were, closed off in that pigeon-infested concrete precinct."

The new site, owned by the Cathedral, had been cleared by the demolition of a nondescript building. Simpson later admitted that his suggestion that the pubs be configured at right angles to fit the space and create a courtyard had been "a bit of a seat of the pants thing," but claims that it worked so well that they look as if they've always been there. Moreover, Ken Riley, the Dean of Manchester and Sir David Trippier, who hadn't been very keen on positioning the pubs so close to the Cathedral, later admitted they were wrong, and the Cathedral got its first ever Visitor Centre out of the deal.

The other key innovation in the Millennium Quarter, though not in itself included in the Masterplan, was Urbis. For all the controversy surrounding the concept of the "museum of the modern city" and its subsequent need of local authority subsidy, Ian Simpson's crystal landmark building which contains it is one of the most striking in the city and he was about to start building his reputation as Manchester's most celebrated architect since Lord Foster. The project swallowed up £30 million of the Millennium Quarter's £42 million budget, funded by the Millennium Commission. Entirely clad in sand-blasted glass, Urbis is as much about knitting the city back together as about creating a landmark tourist attraction.

The site, part of the original Mediaeval city, had been a car park since the Fifties, cut off from the heart of the city by the Arndale Centre. Simpson's masterstroke was to push the building to the edge of the site, leaving room to create Cathedral Gardens beside it, for the first time giving a suitably civic setting to the Cathedral and Chetham's School. The achievement was all the more impressive for the fact that it was only Simpson's second new building. It was also a mark of faith from the city council that it was prepared to take forward such an uncompromising scheme from a relatively untried architect.

Simpson and his partner Rachael Haugh set up their practice in 1987 and the following year appeared in the Royal Institute of British Architects' exhibition of young architects called "40 under 40". Both Urbis and the similarly stunning One Deansgate apartment block, towering above the former Market Place site, were direct results of opportunities presented by the post-bomb reconstruction of Manchester. The firm is now working on projects throughout the country, not least the glass needle-like 46-storey Hilton Tower, dominating Manchester's western skyline.

Their "powerful, reverential" design for a replacement for the World Trade Centre in New York City, destroyed by terrorists on September 11, 2001, reached the semi-final stage of the international competition. Significantly, the bid for that contract highlighted the fact that the firm's "experience in working with local and central government and the lives of ordinary citizens devastated by tragedy made them especially apt candidates".

Cathedral Gardens, a new high-quality public space, of which Manchester has relatively little, is enclosed by the iconic, sleek glass-sided Urbis, the refurbished Edwardian rear façade of the Corn Exchange – re-branded The Triangle following Frogmore Investments' £28 million development of an upmarket shopping complex – and Chetham's School of Music. During the consultation which preceded the launch of the international competition for the Masterplan, the people of Manchester had asked for more trees, greenery and open space. The site of Cathedral Gardens had been a congested, unattractive area long fallen out of favour and had been mostly used as a car park. The people got their wish; lawns sweep down the length of old Fennel Street between the Cathedral and Urbis with cascading water features and a rill channel running the entire length of what had been one of Manchester's oldest streets, Long Millgate.

Simpson's first new building, a foyer project in Birmingham – won against the odds by the only non-London firm as a result of a design competition for young architects - was small scale compared with the landmarks that were to rise on Manchester's skyline. The competition for Manchester's prestigious Millennium project was staged on an anonymous basis. No-one knew the identity of the author of the winning scheme, who was selected from a shortlist of six entries, until the envelopes were opened. On models and maps prepared to illustrate the Masterplan, the proposed cultural building between Corporation Street and Victoria Station had appeared as a rotunda. Simpson's stunning "ski-slope" concept could not have been more different.

Familiar with the Masterplan, after all, its central feature – breaking the city's north-south divide with the creation of New Cathedral Street - had been his original idea, Simpson set out to create a third building that would edge Corporation Street, enclose the new public open space and sit comfortably with the period buildings fronting the other two sides of the triangular site, the Edwardian Corn Exchange and partly-Mediaeval Chetham's School.

He explained: "For the first time, because there had previously been buildings in the way, we were able to appreciate the full elevations of the Corn Exchange and Chetham's, so the idea governing the shape of Urbis was as much about creating the public space that became Cathedral Gardens as the building itself. I wanted a 21st Century building that would respond both to the city and the energy of nearby Exchange Square, so I put the high point facing the curved corners of the Corn Exchange and the Printworks at the bottom of Shudehill, with the form dropping down to respect the scale of the Chetham's buildings.

The competition brief had been to design a flexible series of spaces rather than a showcase for a specific collection or exhibition. It would have been easier for the architect to base his building around a series of objects that would be on permanent view, but Urbis wasn't like that. Simpson continued: "We were trying to create a sense of place and identity without being slaves to exhibits because they were going to be changed frequently. I always felt that the building needed to evolve because what we have to remember is that Urbis is specifically a Millennium project – a massive coup for the city in getting Heseltine to back it – but it meant we couldn't call it a gallery or museum or we wouldn't have got the Heritage Lottery funding for it. So it had to be called something else."

The conclusion has to be that securing the millions for Urbis was another sizeable chunk of Mancunian chutzpah in which the building itself was regarded as far and away more important than its ultimate purpose, an ever-changing exposition of modern city life that even its conceivers has difficulty explaining. Simpson believes that once the rules and regulations governing the award of the grant become "a little less precious", Urbis may be able to present a more formal, conventional gallery and exhibition space. The trick – again - was getting the grant which paid for a critically acclaimed piece of 21st Century architecture – otherwise nothing at all would have happened on this crucial site.

"Not only does Urbis enclose Cathedral Gardens," he observed. "It makes an important link and shifts the weight of the city to the north which I think will lead to major benefits over the next few years. We are seeing development in the Northern Quarter and a major residential scheme at Red Bank, off Cheetham Hill Road; none of that would have happened without this shift. I hope the rippling out of value will enable us to tackle areas that have massive problems of deprivation, poor housing and facilities to the north of the city."

The replaced pillar box with its plaque

Chapter Fifteen

The Leak

DETECTIVE Chief Inspector Gordon Mutch was the police officer handed the task of finding the bombers. Highly respected, very experienced, hugely motivated and well liked, he was the perfect choice to lead the team.

Though a member of Special Branch – the section of a police force that deals with terrorism – he had cut his teeth as a detective working the streets of inner-city Manchester, investigating armed robberies, murders and other major crimes. He was on Detective Chief Superintendent Peter Topping's specialist team that located the body of moors murders victim Pauline Reade on Saddleworth Moor in 1987 and interviewed child killer Myra Hindley during that inquiry. As senior detectives must, he put in gruelling hours. He lived for the job.

Astonishingly, he was also the only person ever charged with a criminal offence in connection with the Manchester bomb.Steve Panter was at the time the chief crime correspondent of the *Manchester Evening News*. Like Mutch, he was vastly experienced and talented at his chosen profession and, remarkably, alongside the policeman, the only other person ever arrested in connection with the events of June 15, 1996.

The pair knew each other well. Mutch appreciated the assistance that the media could provide during an inquiry and actively courted certain journalists he trusted, including Panter. It was not unusual for them to socialise together – it is something crime reporters and police officers do all over the planet as part of their symbiotic relationship. The police and the press have to work together. Without the media, the police would find it much more difficult to solve crimes, and without crime stories the newspapers would sell significantly fewer copies. Moreover, as it is when any groups with basically similar interests get together, albeit coming from different perspectives, acquaintances turn into friendships. Panter and Mutch would have described themselves as friends.

The CID within Greater Manchester Police – more so then than now – was a tight-knit group of men and women who not only worked together but played together. The same faces would be at every party. DCI Mutch liked the socialising side of things and when Panter was invited to an event, the reporter invariably went. The gatherings were always entertaining and it was a key part of Steve's job to mix informally with police, making contacts, digging around for stories.

After one such party early in 1999 – and after overdoing it in terms of beer consumption – the reporter was offered a lift home by another officer, a detective superintendent who, because he was on call, was not drinking and lived not far from Panter. On the way, slurring a little, Steve told him: "I've got a great story. It's the best ever."

"Go on," encouraged the policeman. "What is it?"

"Can't tell you yet, but you'll find out soon."

Panter had the scoop of his career, a guaranteed award winner, and he couldn't wait to get it into print. But he couldn't tell anyone yet, certainly not a policeman, that he had classified documents that pointed to the identity of the man who had organised the Manchester bomb and that the suspect had come to Manchester to case his explosive handiwork and, incredibly, was followed by police as he toured the city's still devastated centre before being allowed to return, unmolested, to his home in South Armagh.

"Thanks for the lift," mumbled Panter, his bushy moustache atop a wide smile; but he was going to have to endure several more weeks of waiting before he could claim credit for his sensational exclusive.

The story was dynamite and the newspaper's editor, Paul Horrocks, understandably wanted to be absolutely certain everything about it was accurate before he would even contemplate publishing. He informed the then Chief Constable, David Wilmot, in February that he had possession of a Special Branch document that detailed the inquiry and its findings and, most dramatic of all, actually named suspects. It also revealed that the police had taken a unilateral decision to keep their evidence secret from Crown lawyers and that, when the Crown Prosecution Service was eventually given sight of it, eighteen months later, they had decided the evidence was too thin to proceed.

Wilmot was incandescent with rage, not so much with the fact of the Evening News getting the document, but with the source. The revelations could have come from only one of two places, the Crown Prosecution Service or, disturbingly for the Chief Constable, from within his own force. But the CPS office they were using for this case was in York for security reasons. Why would a lawyer from York contact the *Manchester Evening News* with sensitive information, particularly when they had deemed it insufficient for them to proceed to trial with any reasonable certainty of getting a conviction?

No; Wilmot was immediately convinced that the source was one of his own officers and he felt personally betrayed. When he first became Chief Constable his force, in his own words, leaked "like a sieve" in terms of information being given to journalists and he had endeavoured to change the culture, with some success. Stories still leaked out, but this, in his opinion, was on a completely different level. It was hugely embarrassing for him and his force as a whole. How could outside agencies now feel comfortable in sharing confidential information with GMP when the organisation couldn't keep its own most sensitive secrets? There and then he decided to find out who was responsible and sanctioned the setting up of a secret incident room whose sole task was to find the 'mole'.

It was headed by a seasoned detective superintendent, Alan Boardman, with an up-and-coming detective inspector, Julian Ross, taking the leading hands-on role. A sergeant and two constables were seconded from their regular duties to make up the team. One was a specialist in surveillance. Interestingly, they were to use techniques during their inquiry identical to some of those deployed during the hunt for the IRA gang.

The newspaper and the chief constable entered into a dialogue over what should and what should not be printed. Certain elements of the sensational story were removed by agreement because the newspaper's bosses accepted those revelations could put officers still engaged in dangerous operations in Ireland in jeopardy. In truth, there was so much startling information in the document that Horrocks could afford to be generous. Just half the available information would create a massive impact. He agreed to put the story on hold to give the police time to consider whether they wanted to arrest the man they had under surveillance, the man who had been the alleged owner of the Digit Six mobile phone, the man about whom the CPS had ruled there was insufficient evidence to enable them to be confident of a conviction.

Six weeks later, with no further news from the police, Horrocks decided he had waited long enough. He considered the story to be too much in the public interest not to publish. Moreover, there was another more mundane, economic reason for putting the story on the front page. The editor took final legal advice and published the revelations over five pages on April 21, 1999, the day the newspaper was re-launched in a new format to try to boost sales.

The Special Branch team that had hunted the bombers was informed of the leak before the story appeared. Everyone in the office they shared expressed shock and disappointment, including Chief Inspector Mutch who, despite his known friendship with the reporter, was considered beyond reproach.

Panter's home and mobile phone may or may not have been tapped, but his telephone records were certainly seized and scrutinised, as were his finances, in an effort to see if he had paid for his information. The phone records showed contact between him and a number of police officers, including Mutch, which, in itself, was not too significant as he was a busy crime reporter. But the mole hunters also managed to place both men's telephones at a hotel in Skipton, Yorkshire, on the same evening. The investigation team's own visit to the hotel confirmed Panter and Mutch had stayed there overnight a couple of weeks before the newspaper had informed the police about their information. Dark clouds of suspicion were beginning to gather. Why would the scoop-hungry journalist and the leader of the bomb investigation team need a clandestine meeting 40 miles from Manchester?

The answer, the investigators felt, was obvious. The leaked information was contained in a large document; it would have taken time to go through the details. Some of it might be unclear to a non-policeman, albeit a civilian with a lot of experience of working with the police. Further, they were often seen together in Manchester, it was not unusual and there would be no reason for suspicions to be raised. This time, though, the stakes were too high to risk being spotted.

Gordon Mutch was visited by police officers at his home on June 28, 1999, arrested in front of his family under the Official Secrets Act and brought in for questioning. He was treated exactly like any suspect in a serious crime, notwithstanding his status as a senior police officer, held overnight and questioned thoroughly the following day. Finally, he was released without charge, but suspended from duty on full pay. It would be another two years and six months before he worked again.

In November 1999 Steve Panter was also arrested – ironically the day before the celebratory opening of Exchange Square, a milestone in the post-bomb reconstruction of the city - and questioned at length by Ross and the "mole squad" about his source. Pressure was put on him to reveal who gave him the documents but, while later he admitted it was a terrifying experience, he remained firmly silent over the issue, claiming a journalist's duty to protect sources. He was never charged with any offence.

When Mutch answered his bail, however, he was charged with "misconduct in a public office" an offence which can carry a jail term. When the case came to court Panter was subpoenaed as a witness for the defence. He had told police in a statement that Mutch was not his source but he knew that this assertion was bound to be challenged when he took the oath and gave evidence in court. He further knew that when he repeated in the witness box that Mutch was not his 'mole' he would be asked to identify the person who was. If Mutch's defence lawyers elicited the name of another suspect, their client would be in the clear.

Here lay Panter's problem. If he was lying and the Special Branch Chief Inspector was indeed the source of the leaked list of terror suspects, then there was no-one else he could name. If he were to put anyone else in the frame then he would be fingering someone who played no part in the whole matter and that was a non-starter. Ethics aside, it simply couldn't work.

But if he was telling the truth and Mutch was not the man, then he had to make a big decision. If Gordon, his friend, was innocent, and Panter had incontrovertible evidence of that fact, then, in any other circumstances, he would be honour-bound to divulge that evidence and save the wrongly accused man from a potential jail term. But to do so would reveal the identity of the individual who was the source who, clearly, would face similar sanction to that which Mutch had been subjected. Whom should he sacrifice, his friend or his accomplice?

Then there was a third factor. It is cut deep into the psyche of serious journalists that their sources, should they wish to remain anonymous, should always be able to do so. It is a pre-requisite for any investigative reporter. Any other situation would mean that journalists' sources would dry up and the profession would be unable to deliver an investigative process at any level. In short, if people passing on information thought they would be identified, they would not deliver.

A source's anonymity is sacrosanct and the level of his invisibility rises in direct correlation to the importance of the story. This was the biggest story of Panter's career. He couldn't buckle, he decided, whatever the pressure. And the pressure now was much more than he had endured under the interrogation of DI Ross and his men. He was going to have to stand up in court and in all probability face down a top QC and a judge with the power to send him to jail at no notice. Later, in an article for the *Manchester Evening News*, he recalled the days before the trial began at Manchester Crown Court.

"In my mind I had all but packed, ready to go to jail," he wrote. "I had, literally, put my house in order. Why else would I have spent a month painting my home inside and out? This was more than therapy for the torment plaguing my waking hours and keeping me sleepless at night. My whole family was engulfed by my personal calamity.

"There was an awful moment when my young daughter was reading out loud from a huge Harry Potter book. She paused and said: 'Don't worry, dad. If I don't finish this before you go to prison, I'll read you the rest when you come out.'"

Mutch's eleven-day trial was heard in January 2002; the detective pleaded not guilty, the prosecution stacked up a large amount of circumstantial evidence against him with high powered witnesses, including Chief Constable Wilmot, and it didn't look good.

The Crown's trump card was that though the defence now accepted that the two men had spent nearly 24 hours together at the hotel in Skipton, with Panter paying for both the lodgings and their food, neither, when first questioned, had mentioned it to the investigators. Surely, argued the prosecution, if this had been an innocent meeting, unconnected to the IRA inquiry, both men would have offered explanations for their connivance straight away?

In court both men insisted that their meeting had been to discuss the possibility of collaborating on a book about the Moors Murders using Gordon Mutch's experience of the Topping inquiry, his knowledge of Myra Hindley, and the fact it was 25 years on since the creation of Greater Manchester Police from an amalgamation of parts of the old shire forces. Panter had already written one book about another child murder so would be qualified to ghost-write the policeman's memoirs, they argued.

Mutch explained that he did not reveal that he had met the reporter shortly before the IRA revelations because he was in a "Catch 22" situation. "I was very, very frightened," he said. "I took the view I would say nothing and hopefully the matter would be resolved." He was worried that his meeting with the reporter would be "misconstrued".

Panter said he did not mention the meeting in his earlier interviews with police simply because he was advised not to by lawyers appointed by his newspaper.

The reporter was the star witness for the defence, marshalled by the eminent barrister Peter Wright, QC. At first everything was straightforward.

"Was Mr Mutch your source?" the lawyer probed.

"No," Panter replied.

"Did he tell you anything of a confidential nature during your meeting in Skipton?"

"No."

"In the interests of justice, would you tell the court the identity of your source?" It was a fair question from a defence lawyer determined to have his client cleared without a stain on his record.

Panter: "No."

The journalist spent more than a day in the witness box having this same question repeated in a variety of ways from all the barristers and, most crucially, the judge, Mr Justice Leveson, QC. Despite being traumatised by the experience, Panter remained steadfast in his refusal to say more.

"Do you appreciate the potential consequences of this course of action?" asked the judge.

"Yes, your Honour," replied a now quite petrified reporter desperately trying to stop shaking.

Slowly, deliberately, the judge explained that if the law was satisfied that disclosing a source was in the interests of justice, a court could "require" a journalist to disclose that source, overriding the principle of journalistic confidence which he nevertheless recognised was "very important" in a democratic society.

"The disclosure of your source is a necessity in this case and you should answer relevant and material questions," he demanded.

Once more, and for the last time, Panter refused. Exasperated, Mr Justice Leveson, QC, finally declared the journalist was in contempt of court, a point at which Panter remembered his daughter and Harry Potter.

The jury cleared Gordon Mutch after three hours of deliberation and he broke down in the dock and wept with relief.

However, he was told that because he had brought suspicion upon himself by not declaring his "innocent" meeting with the reporter in Skipton, he would have to pay £10,000 towards his own defence costs. He spent several weeks off duty, suffering from stress brought on by the whole set of events, before returning to work for GMP. Subsequently, he said that, apart from a handful of close friends, none of his former colleagues treated him the same again, despite his acquittal, and he retired from the force shortly afterwards having completed his 30 years service. It was a tragic end to a distinguished career, irrespective of his guilt or innocence.

The judge could have jailed Panter for a significant period as soon as he was satisfied that a contempt had been committed and in those instant judgements, an erring witness has no right of appeal. In the interests of justice, however, His Honour decided instead to invite the Attorney General to consider charging the reporter with contempt, such a charge being subject to an appeal. The stay of execution, while welcome in the short term, served to pile the anxieties on to the reporter. It was another six months before the Attorney General decided such a trial would not be in the public interest and ended Panter's ordeal, though he was left shattered by his experience.

Inevitably, in view of the failure of the police to bring any of the bombers to justice, there was political fallout from the case with politicians queuing up to criticise both the prosecution of the policeman and the pursuit of a journalist who was just doing his job. The not guilty verdict on the charges brought against Mutch, and the Attorney General's decision not to take matters facing Panter any further gave weight to the view that the prosecution had been a waste of time and money.

Graham Stringer, MP for Blackley, said: "It was a ridiculous decision to even consider bringing a prosecution. It is a good day for the freedom of the Press."

Manchester Evening News editor, Paul Horrocks, added: "I have always maintained this was a story the people of Manchester had a right to know. We are now left with a situation where the police identified a suspect but there was no prosecution. Instead they chose to investigate a suspected leak and charged a police officer. Steve also suffered a terrible ordeal; he was arrested, interrogated, and his financial records were probed. It took great personal strength for him not to reveal his source when ordered to do so by the judge. He was standing by our basic code of journalism and we are proud of him. The public must be able to trust us not to reveal confidential sources unless there are exceptional circumstances."

Steve Panter was promoted from crime correspondent to news editor but then left the *Manchester Evening News* to teach a university course in journalism.

Chapter Sixteen

The Show Goes On

FOR those who were living and working in Manchester, few periods in the city's history could have been more exciting and dynamic than the five years between 1997 and 2002. As the rebuilding progressed, each phase being unveiled amid fanfare and fireworks, the sense of pride, achievement and resilience among Mancunians grew. It would be a new and confident city that presented itself to the world's inquisitive gaze for the Commonwealth Games. It was an extraordinary time; the task force charged with the reconstruction and the team engaged in the organisation of the biggest multi-sports tournament in the UK's history were working at opposite ends of the same room but with a common aim.

When Michael Heseltine addressed his audience at the Bridgewater Hall by live video link on February 10th 1997 to unveil a further £43 millon government aid package to seed the reconstruction effort, he described the gathering mood exactly by saying: "This is the most exciting thing to happen to Manchester this century". He was right. Howard Bernstein, in what turned out to be a modest estimate, reckoned the injection of government capital money would lever in £500 million from the private sector. "We did our sums very carefully and we were able to present a case to government with which they could not argue," he said. Cranes towered above vast cleared building sites in the heart of the city, fenced off from the hustle and bustle of street life but offering tantalising glimpses of a new centre rising from its foundations.

But huge schemes were under way or beginning all over Manchester. The Great Northern Initiative, encapsulating the city's long-time ambition to regenerate the old Great Northern Railway's massive goods warehouse and canal-rail interchange that had dominated the western end of Deansgate for 100 years, was at last progressing through the planning process in 1997. It was an all-embracing scheme hanging over from the mid-1980s intended to expand the city's tourism and leisure facilities, provide jobs and secure inward investment. Important in its own right, given the scale of the ten-acre site in a prime location, the project was also a key component in a much grander plan to create a business, conference and leisure district close to the Edwardian landmark Midland Hotel, the just-completed Bridgewater Hall and the G-Mex exhibition centre – itself a conversion of the train hall of the Midland Railway and Cheshire Lines' former terminal station, Manchester Central.

Chief Superintendent Harris introduces the evacuation heroes to Her Majesty

The £100 million metamorphosis of the GNR warehouse, unused for half a century, was undertaken by Morrison Developments and Merlin International Properties in conjunction with English Partnerships and involved the controversial demolition of a Grade II listed carriage ramp and some of the listed railway viaduct and buildings in Peter Street. In their place, Great Northern Square, with its attractive open-air amphitheatre and cascading water feature, became Manchester's first new public square since the Second World War. In fact the scheme was essentially a compromise; grandiose early plans for a shopping centre in the huge brick building were dropped; the megalithic centre building mostly houses a 1,200-space car park whilst still boasting 500,000 square feet of shops, bars, restaurants and cinemas. The multiplex, cinema, however, struggled in the face of competition from the Printworks entertainment complex in the former Daily Mirror newspaper printing plant much closer to the bomb blast site.

The cornerstone of the Great Northern strategy turned out to be new-build – the Manchester International Conference Centre, the UK's first purpose-built convention complex linked directly to an exhibition centre and located in a city centre. The £29 million MICC was funded by Manchester City Council, English Partnerships and the European Regional Development Fund and has, since completion in 2000, attracted many prestigious national and international conferences. Arguably the most important was the Labour Party's spring conference of 2005 which proved to be a "dry run" for the main party conference to be staged in the heart of one of Britain's major cities rather than at a seaside location such as Blackpool, Bournemouth or Brighton for the first time in decades.

Staging conferences of that size, however – upwards of 20,000 delegates, media representatives, exhibitors, lobbyists and visitors – required not just state-of-the-art convention facilities, but hotel accommodation and it was this that underpinned the rationale for the city council's approval of a scheme to turn the city's Free Trade Hall into a luxury hotel. If demolition of listed facets of the Great Northern Warehouse attracted controversy, proposals for a building so central to the political and social history of the city caused a storm of protest.

In truth, however, the Free Trade Hall, despite its past and location on the site of the Peterloo Massacre of 1819, had become a major liability and, once the Hallé Orchestra had moved to its new home in the Bridgewater Hall after 150 years in the Peter Street building, effectively redundant. Moreover very little of the original structure, rebuilt in 1856 in the classic Palazzo style as the home of Manchester's free trade movement, survived the Luftwaffe's Second World War bombing raid that left one and a half facades standing and the interior completely gutted. The fact that the reconstructed building, opened in the austerity year of 1951, was rather functional, was of little avail amid the outcry over its future.

This was the scene where Gladstone addressed an audience in 1862; Charles Dickens made annual appearances and in 1907 Winston Churchill was heckled by suffragettes. The explorer H M Stanley lectured on 'geographical science' in 1884, some thirteen years after presuming to find Dr Livingstone. One day in May 1865, the whole of the interior was draped in black for a memorial service to the assassinated Abraham Lincoln. And 101 years later Bob Dylan famously sparked another outburst of mourning when he picked up an electric guitar and played rock and roll to a shout of "traitor" from the audience.

The first planning application by developers La Sande was submitted on behalf of the Millennium Copthorne Hotels in 1997 followed by a second design which, following objections led by the Manchester Civic Society, forced a public inquiry in 1998. When this was in turn rejected by the Secretary of State, a third version emerged that was accepted and work eventually began on what became Radisson Edwardian's £40 million project in 2002.

"Missed the matinée, should be on tonight" – that piece of monumental bravado emanating from the Royal Exchange Theatre hours after the explosion of the bomb, less than 60 yards away, proved well wide of the mark despite the damage only appearing superficial. It took almost two and a half years and £32 million of Arts Council/National Lottery aid before the curtain was raised again at the pioneering theatre in the round.

Halle Square, In the redesigned Arndale Centre

Cross Street 2006

While its home was being rebuilt, the company had performed in its mobile theatre, set up in the indoor Upper Campfield Market in Castlefield, almost a mile away. Such was the scale and complexity of the building, it took almost a year to assess the damage and the news wasn't good. But the steely determination that the show would eventually go on was voiced by actress Una Stubbs, who had been in rehearsal at the theatre at the time of the blast and, with other cast members, was forced to flee for her life. "The Royal Exchange has a very special place in many actors' hearts," she declared. "It is as beloved as the National in London. No-one wanted to see the place die."

The theatre was given a royal reopening on November 30th 1998 by Prince Edward, Earl of Wessex, and fittingly the first comeback production was Stanley Houghton's play, Hindle Wakes, whose run in 1996 had been so rudely interrupted by the IRA bombers. As well as repairing the theatre, the rebuilding programme also added a second performance space with 100 seats called The Studio, a bookshop, craft shop, restaurant, bars, and rooms for corporate hospitality. The theatre's workshops, costume department and rehearsal rooms were moved to a second site on Swan Street. To mastermind the refurbishment, the Royal Exchange went back to the original architects, Levitt Bernstein. Inside the main theatre space, the clarity of the design was reinstated with stunning colours; sound and lighting systems were all upgraded and new air conditioning was installed.

In the public spaces of the grand hall, unplanned additions were reorganised and bars, cafes, shops and entertainment areas renewed, all dramatically revealed by a new lighting scheme. Backstage, similar far-reaching improvements were effected in dressing rooms, rehearsal, sound recording, office and backstage support spaces, squeezed into the perimeter of the building.

"It would be wrong to say that without the lottery money we would have closed forever," said Pat Weller, executive director of the theatre. "We did have insurance. But without lottery support, our re-launch would have been basic and uninteresting." Instead, as the Royal Exchange was the first of the city centre's damaged landmarks to reopen – ahead of Marks & Spencer, the Printworks and the Triangle, the theatre came to symbolise the whole centre of Manchester getting back into business.

Manchester learned to enjoy a party and there were many. Thousands turned out for each phase of the city's reopening. And if that wasn't enough, an estimated 700,000 people took to the city's streets on 27th May 1999 to greet Manchester United's treble-winning heroes after they returned from Barcelona with the Champions League trophy. Their last-gasp extra-time comeback against Bayern Munich to win the match 2-1 – the team had already clinched the FA Cup and the Premiership title – was the stuff of legend. Riding in an open-top bus the players paraded all three trophies to fans thronging the city centre from Castlefield to the Manchester Evening News Arena where 17,500 tickets had been sold for the celebration, passing on the way the still-cordoned off core where the bomb had exploded. At first the club had been reluctant to stage the parade amid fears over security, but after meetings with Manchester city council and their neighbours in Trafford, the stage was set for what Pat Karney, co-organiser as chairman of Manchester's city centre committee, described as "the parade of parades; the greatest street party the city has ever seen."

Six months later, Mancunians were out in force again, this time saluting the team that had delivered the promises made amid the mayhem after the blast, as the wraps came off their handiwork. Thousands of people assembled amid a carnival atmosphere outside the town hall in Albert Square before walking down Cross Street to the pulsating rhythm of throbbing drums. "We're back," people yelled as they advanced along Cross Street and into Corporation Street, past the very spot where the IRA's lorry had exploded into smithereens. On the crowd surged, young and old, into Exchange Square, the pivotal feature of the redesigned city, where, despite torrential rain, trapeze artists and acrobats swung from cranes and a huge broadside of fireworks burst with spectacular pyrotechnic florescence over the rooftop of the biggest Marks & Spencer store in the world.

Exchange Square, a new public space in the form of an acute triangle, bounded by Marks & Spencer, the relocated Shambles pubs and the regenerating Corn Exchange, with the Printworks taking shape across the road and a huge flat mural heralding the transformation of the Arndale North, was a fitting focal point for the celebrations, a role it assumed for many later events, from the Proms to the Commonwealth Games. The site had been, before its post-bomb demolition, partly occupied by Longridge House, the seriously damaged Royal Insurance Building and heavily trafficked, particularly by buses, along both Cateaton Street and Hanging Ditch. Now they are gone, replaced by American Martha Schwartz's radical design featuring a series of gentle ramps linking the square's two levels with the ancient watercourse of Hanging Ditch "reinvented" as a stream gushing from water heads and racing between stone channels.

Interestingly, the most bizarre element of the original design never made it from the drawing board to reality. When the first artists' impressions of the new-look space were revealed, they contained serried ranks of stylised fake palm trees. Amid an outbreak of mild derision, the idea of the faux forest was felled, but Exchange Square still contains a few surprises: flange-wheel trucks mounted on short lengths of track and designer John Hyatt's tall, slow-turning metallic "windmills" whose lazy animation reflects to delightful effect in the glass façade of what is now the Selfridge's half of the Marks & Spencer store. In recent times Exchange Square has also been the site of The Wheel of Manchester, the 365-tonne, 200-feet-tall Ferris wheel affording panoramic views of the rebuilt city centre and beyond from its 42 heated glass gondolas.

In August 2000 there were more celebrations when the Corn Exchange re-emerged from behind the screens after its £28 million refurbishment as The Triangle, a galleried shopping venue whose "alternative" traders had given way to designer stores and chic restaurants. The dramatic transformation that took place beneath the restored soaring glass dome wasn't to everyone's liking; many of the building's Edwardian period features had been obscured by the makeover, but Mancunians were grateful that the grand old lady of Hanging Ditch had survived. The party moved across the road barely three months later as the Printworks made its spectacular debut.

Manchester's claim to be England's second city was never based on population, which was always smaller than Birmingham's – and indeed Liverpool's – and now, at 400,000 (as opposed to Greater Manchester's 2.5m) ranks no higher than eighth in the UK. It was all about influence, of which the most important element was the concentration of media interests. The BBC's decision to switch 1,800 staff to Manchester will make the city the Corporation's biggest outpost outside London and its local independent television company, Granada, swallowed up all its rivals to create a single ITV. But that is recent history; it was the city's eminence as a newspaper production centre that gave Manchester its clout. Almost all the national titles maintained large editorial staffs and printing facilities in the city centre and the influence of its own newspaper, the Manchester Guardian, was international. There were several printing plants in the city and the Withy Grove Press was the biggest of its kind in Europe. In the 1980s, the building was acquired by newspaper tycoon Robert Maxwell, and used to produce his publications, including The Mirror; but change was under way within the industry at an accelerating pace; in 1986, Withy Grove produced its last paper and from 1987, the site stood derelict. Nine years later, it sustained severe damage when the bomb exploded 500 yards along Corporation Street.

A derelict, bomb-damaged printing plant of no particular architectural merit did not, on the face of it, appear to present much in the way of a regeneration project, but Birmingham-based Richardson Developments, run by twin brother founders Don and Roy, thought otherwise and bought the site for £10 million. Their vision was the creation of a US-style entertainments centre; its 500,000 square foot area providing a 20-screen cinema and the biggest 3-D Imax theatre in Europe, supported by 34 bars and fifteen restaurants, including Manchester's own Hard Rock Café. The Printworks would open 24 hours a day and have a capacity of 25,000 people.

In consultation with the Withy Grove Fellowship, whose members are retired press employees, architect David Gester followed a design brief to recreate the flavour of the original building, whilst incorporating elements of New York. Work commenced in January 1998 with the demolition of the main part of the building to basement level behind the retained façade. Individual tenants called in their own structural design teams in a bid to put their own stamp on the building. As a result, The Printworks houses an eclectic range of venues, attractive to visitors of all ages, interests and origins.

The opening on 9th November saw Sir Alex Ferguson kick a football through a goalmouth beneath a stage erected in Withy Grove and the star performer was the legendary American singer, Lionel Ritchie. It wasn't exactly hard rock, but the spectacle of a multi-million selling recording artist playing in a Manchester street was typically off the wall. The fusillade of celebratory fireworks over central Manchester had by now become a regular occurrence in the Millennium year's night sky.

Chapter Seventeen

Faster Higher Stronger

THE task of preparing for the biggest multi-sport event ever staged in Britain ran parallel to the reconstruction of Manchester city centre in the years following the IRA bomb, and the spectacular staging of the Commonwealth Games in Kuala Lumpur in 1998 had set the bar higher. The Malaysians had seen the event as a statement of national prestige; the attitude of many British commentators to Manchester's games was, in complete contrast, highly sceptical. In the first place the Commonwealth Games had been a second best following the city's failed bids for the Olympic Games of 1996 and 2000. Those initiatives too had attracted derision in sections of the London-centric media, who argued that only London was capable of making a successful bid. Comments from within the International Olympic Committee later appeared to echo that view, but flew in the face of the facts; since the modern Olympics began in Athens in 1896, the games have been staged 24 times, and on nearly half of those occasions – eleven to be precise - in non-capital cities.

Moreover, Manchester's Commonwealth Games' planning was taking place amid chronic failure in London to do anything right. The £800 million cost of the Millennium Dome in Greenwich was a self-indulgent national disgrace as was the on-going scandal over the ever-escalating cost of the new Wembley Stadium. London had been humiliated in international sporting circles in 2001 by defaulting on its commitment to stage the 2005 World Athletics Championships because there was no suitable venue, the government having wisely calculated that the provision of another stadium at Pickett's Lock would be politically unacceptable in view of the Wembley debacle. The futile bid to stage the World Cup in 2006, doomed before it started, wasted another £10 million. Just as well, for the north London money pit was not ready, despite repeated pledges, to stage the 2006 FA Cup final.

Wembley's embarassment over what had become a £750 million national disgrace was further compounded at the end of March 2006 when the stadium's bosses announced that no events, sporting or otherwise, would be staged there until 2007. Scheduled concerts by pop music giants The Rolling Stones, Bon Jovi, Take That and Robbie Williams had all to be switched away from the unfinished venue. Even the Football Association was forced to admit that its pet project was in trouble and it was clear that the construction of Wembley was 'significantly behind schedule'. The mood in Manchester was one of *schadenfreude* at London's acute discomfort and that of the F.A. who were still held to have cheated the city in the contest to build the national stadium. It was a very public comeuppance for a very underhand trick.

Manchester's motive for bagging the Commonwealth Games, however, was not primarily based on sporting factors, nor on civic prestige. Like the 2000 Olympic bid, the aim was to use the facilities and their legacy as one of the key drivers for the regeneration of east Manchester. Working towards the 2002 games provided the underlying theme against which to justify bids for a wide range of regeneration programmes. The task of regenerating east Manchester was and remains one of the most challenging in the UK and its comprehensive, integrated and long-term nature makes it unique.

The area was once the economic powerhouse of the city, home to traditional industries from coal mining and steel production to textiles, chemicals and engineering. Decline between 1970 and 1985 was catastrophic and what had once been the workshop of the world was identified as one of the poorest and most disadvantaged places in Britain.

The vision for east Manchester, stretching from Ancoats, the world's first industrial suburb on the edge of the city centre, through Miles Platting, Newton Heath, Beswick, Openshaw, Clayton, Ardwick and Gorton to the city's boundary, is that it will become stable and successful again. But so large is the area and so complex and comprehensive the renewal required, that it is one of only four places in the country to have its own urban regeneration company. New East Manchester Limited owes much to the city's experience of forging partnerships with key players to deliver successful outcomes, from Hulme to the reconstruction of the city centre. NEM, launched in 2001, drew together the city council, English Partnerships and the North West Development Agency and forged a long-term framework for redevelopment, building on activities already under way.

The company's first chairman was Sir Alan Cockshaw, then chairman of English Partnerships and a very familiar name from his stint on the city centre task force, Manchester Millennium Ltd, which had produced its final report the year before. When Cockshaw retired in 2003, his place was taken by another seasoned player, Robert Hough, chairman and managing director of the Manchester Ship Canal Company, previously joint chairman of Manchester 2002, the organisers of the Commonwealth Games. Hough had also been one of the earliest private sector contacts with Manchester city council's left wing leaders during their "learning curve" in the mid-1980s.

East Manchester's £2 billion agenda is immense; by 2014 the many partners, public and private, will oversee the development of more than 12,500 new homes, the improvement of 7,000 existing ones, a doubling of the population to 60,000 and the creation of 15,000 new jobs. Through the creation of Central Park, the UK's first mixed-use urban business park, the regeneration of the area is aimed at creating 10,000 jobs in a period of ten to fifteen years.

While the ambition to drive forward the vast regeneration programme never wavered, the road to hosting the XVII Commonwealth Games proved to be a rocky one. Overseeing the delivery process was Manchester 2002 Limited, chaired by Charles Allen, then also the chairman of Granada Television, with Frances Done as Chief Executive and Howard Bernstein playing the critical liaison role on behalf of Manchester city council who were underwriting the event and to whom, in the event of a deficit, the chickens would come home to roost.

Even on the eve of the Manchester event, memories were dredged up of the deficit run up by the 1986 Commonwealth Games in Edinburgh and the £22 million annual debt burden still being carried by Sheffield city council from the 1991 World Student Games. The Commonwealth Games Federation itself admitted that no modern games where operating costs had to be met by private finance had made a profit. There was no lack of scare stories about the completion of the main venue either - the most persistent being alleged problems caused by old mine workings from the demolished Bradford pit nearby. But East Manchester's showpiece, SportCity, with the City of Manchester Stadium at its centre, was rising majestically from the former industrial wastelands.

It was not until 2001, after concerted and lengthy behind-the-scenes lobbying that a formal tripartite funding agreement was signed between the government, through the Department for Culture, Media and Sport, Manchester city council and Sport England that at last established a strong financial footing for the staging of a successful Games. It had been a hair-raising ride and Bernstein admitted: "The Manchester games were viewed with considerable cynicism outside the city, people didn't believe we could do it. I always believed we could – and we did. The media did give us a hard time, but I don't think the scepticism really got into the consciousness of the general public. As far as the government was concerned, I think they saw Manchester as being opportunistic in that we'd bid for one thing and, after the scale of the Commonwealth Games in Kuala Lumpur, had decided to stage something else."

Frances Done, the imaginative former chair of Manchester town hall's finance committee had a reputation for financial management and connections with the city of Manchester which made her the ideal candidate to take charge of Manchester 2002 at a time when the ship needed steadying. When she was headhunted for the position in the autumn of 1999, however, she had little idea of the helter-skelter experience to come.

"I was completely gob-smacked to be recruited for the role," she said later. "I couldn't imagine why anyone would think I could do it. But once I did think about it I began to understand why I had been asked. Of course, I was thinking: 'Sport? I don't know anything about sport.' Rochdale, where I was Chief Executive of the council at the time, may be only about ten miles north of Manchester but it's a long way from Manchester politics."

Done had not been associated with any of the Olympic or Commonwealth Games bids, so all she knew about the Commonwealth Games was that they were probably a good thing. It didn't take to long for her to discover that Manchester's real agenda went far beyond ten days of international sport but there was a snag – a looming budget deficit variously estimated by speculative press reports at anywhere between £20 million and £68 million.

"I didn't know there was a hole in the budget, no one told me. But I could have guessed, couldn't I?" she recalled. "Let's just say I wasn't shocked."

Even years after the games Done is unwilling to disclose the extent of the crisis. "In any case," she insisted, "it all came out in the wash". Despite the budget gap, Howard Bernstein, by now the Chief Executive of Manchester city council, was convinced that at some stage the government would have to step in like the cavalry coming over the hill and rescue what was a national event. It did precisely that in the diminutive shape of Ian McCartney, MP for Makerfield and Cabinet Office Secretary, who was given responsibility for co-ordinating government departments to ensure the delivery of the Games.

"It depends on how you look at it," said Done. "I know it all turned out alright in the end but there was a real 'nothing ventured, nothing gained' element about these things. It was the way Howard worked. And as a result of what Manchester did, the staging of prestigious national sporting events will never happen like that again. The Olympic bid was completely underwritten by the government, which is how the Commonwealth Games should have been handled from the outset, rather than leaving the onus on the host city."

The original budget for the Commonwealth Games was just £68 million. The actual cost of staging the event, including the provision of the sporting venues, was £276 million. There had been consternation when McCartney told MPs on the Culture, Media and Sport select committee that there would be no more government money for the staging of the games beyond that which had already been provided to procure the venues. In the end, however, he delivered additional support in excess of £60 million, providing a final tranche of support for the stadium and funds for the spectacular opening and closing ceremonies. The contention that the last-ditch injection of cash "almost certainly saved the games" as the culture committee claimed, is arguable. Did the games have to be "bailed out" or was Manchester 2002's high wire act a deliberate device to procure extra funding for an event of which the nation could be proud?

Done, like most of the most influential figures in Manchester, naturally took the latter view. "In the end we sorted it out, but if the extra money had not been forthcoming to bridge the gap and make the games the event they needed to be – and with hindsight that was absolutely right – then we would have had to scale it down. There was no question that we could have run the Commonwealth Games for a lot less. By coincidence I was in Victoria when the 1994 Games were staged in Canada and it was a very low key event. The truth is that Manchester did not have the reserves and could not have put masses of money into the Games, so we just wouldn't have done it. We would have found another way, which is really why someone like me had to get involved; first because of my commitment to the city; second because someone had to be able to understand why it all really mattered to us – the massive task of regenerating east Manchester.

"You couldn't have been a prima donna; it had to be 'somehow we've got to find our way through this' and that's how we operated really. It was a real seat of the pants job but it was a good outcome. Ian McCartney was great; there were lots of efforts going on; you never quite knew what the exact thing was that made it all work, but it worked. If it hadn't, there was no way we would have left the city in a financial mess. The whole thing would have been on a lesser scale."

So was it a rewarding experience? "After the event," she said.

Despite the commitment of extra funding, the amount of money Manchester got from the government for the Commonwealth Games was smaller than what the government gave to London just for the privilege of bidding for the Olympics. Bernstein said: "God knows what the cost of staging 2012 will be but it will be a lot more than £2.5 billion. While I was absolutely delighted that London won, it's a pity that the choice of British representative was made without competition. I think they would have had more support from the rest of the country had that been so."

Bernstein said he believed that the organisers of the London games are bound to ride the same roller-coaster that Manchester's 2002 team did and might learn from their predecessors.

"At no stage in that process did we lose a single corporate or community associate," he said. "That was because they all saw the complete and total relationship between what we were trying to do with the Commonwealth Games and how we wanted to see our city change for the future. The residents of Manchester understood that; the business community, everybody. So yes we were getting a lot of crap from London and the south east's media, but never locally. For the most part we saw the delivery of the Commonwealth Games as an absolute must."

Richard Leese, the city council leader who would have carried the political can for failure, said: "There was a lot riding on the Games. The delivery of such a world class event was not only crucial to the economic and social development of Manchester and the North West, but also to the nation's ability to bid for and stage sporting and cultural events of global significance."

The contribution of Manchester's Commonwealth Games success to London's decision to bid for the 2012 Olympic Games and its sensational triumph in winning the race to stage them is, nevertheless, debatable. There are some parallels between Manchester's determination to use sport to regenerate east Manchester and the benefits that will accrue from basing the Olympics in Statford, the run-down district in east London. But Bernstein said the approach was completely different. London did not need the Olympic Games to regenerate.

"There are some parts of the capital that need regenerating which, in the absence of the Olympics, the authorities might have had difficulty in promoting, but for the most part London is the last place in the country that needs the Olympic Games from the perspective of regeneration. It is very wealthy, one of the most successful cities in the world, and it's because it is a success story that the Olympics have been awarded to London. I think they should not be afraid to say that – but I do think the Games' long-term legacy should be related not just to London, but how we drive long-term sporting achievement throughout the country."

If there was one occasion when the pride of regenerated Manchester city centre and the fever-pitch excitement generated by the imminent Commonwealth Games conjoined, it was during the afternoon and evening of July 24th 2002. A special Thanksgiving Service for the "Miracle of Manchester" at Manchester Cathedral attended by the Queen and Prince Philip coincided with the arrival in the city of the Commonwealth Games' baton after its 85-day global relay through 24 countries. Manchester's prayer, read during the service by the Lord Mayor, Roy Walters, to a congregation of more than 1,000, never sounded so apposite.

"Oh God, grant us a vision of our city, fair as it might be. A city of justice, where none shall prey on others; a city of plenty, where vice and poverty shall cease to fester; a city in community, where success shall be founded on service and honour given to worth alone; a city of peace where order shall not rest on force, but on the love of all for the city. Hear, oh Lord, the silent prayer of all our hearts as we each pledge our time, strength and thought to speed the day of her coming beauty and righteousness. Amen."

It was a lump-in-the-throat occasion for all of those who had seen the scenes of untold damage 200 yards away just six years before. The Queen and Prince Philip were joined by leaders of the city council and of the neighbouring authorities, personnel from the task force that led the rebuilding programme, and the emergency services who had evacuated the area around the bomb. During the service the Archbishop of York, the Most

Reverend David Hope, paid tribute to Manchester as "a great northern city" which had successfully translated its imaginative planning strategy into impressive achievement, and to the community of people who had made the day possible. He emphasised the "very happy co-incidence" that had aligned the Commonwealth Games with the Queen's Golden Jubilee.

The then Bishop of Manchester, the Right Reverend Christopher Mayfield, said that generations of immigration in the city over the centuries meant that the city's communities "included the world." It was a diversity that added richness and strength to a great city which should be celebrated, and the Commonwealth Games would bring even stronger relationships. In what was an ecumenical occasion, the Roman Catholic Bishop of Salford, the Right Reverend Thomas Brain, added: "Through the confidence, commitment and co-operation of so many, a great evil had been overcome by good; Manchester has emerged from the ashes of destruction."

During the service the Queen was presented with a replica of the original Masterplan for the rebuilding of the city and handed it to the Dean of Manchester, the Very Reverend Ken Riley, for safe keeping in the Cathedral archives. The Sovereign was also given a lighted candle which she passed on to a child, symbolising the handing on of her personal commitment to service from one generation to another. Afterwards, the royals engaged in a familiar "walkabout" in Exchange Square and opened the Cathedral's new Visitor Centre.

The arrival of the Commonwealth Games baton – doubling as the Queen's Jubilee baton - in Manchester's Albert Square, last stop but one on a journey that had begun in London on March 14, was greeted by a crowd of almost 20,000. It was held aloft on its way to the square by footballers Ryan Giggs of Manchester United and Stuart Pearce, then a Manchester City player, later the club's manager. Manchester on that day was a city united. Crowds also gathered in Exchange Square where they watched entertainers including a gospel choir, Aboriginal dancers and South African drummers by live video feed from Albert Square. The footballers placed the baton, containing a message from the Queen which she was to read out at the opening ceremony of the Games, on a plinth which was then raised upwards and surrounded by fireworks. The message had been put there at Buckingham Palace at the start of its 60,000 mile journey by the first person to carry it, the first man in history to run a mile in under four minutes, Sir Roger Bannister.

Giggs said: "I was delighted to be asked to carry the baton; this is the place where I grew up and this is a great event, so I hope everyone enjoys it." Pearce revealed he was looking forward to attending the Games at the stadium which, the following year, would be the new home of Manchester City following the club's switch from their old Maine Road ground in Moss Side. "My chairman has offered me the use of his hospitality box," quipped the defender. "So I'll be taking him up on that next week."

The baton's final leg of the journey, from Manchester town hall to the City of Manchester Stadium, would be earlier: at 0555 BST on Thursday 25th July. By any measure, Manchester's Commonwealth Games proved to be a triumph, not just in sporting terms but for the city as a whole. Television coverage abroad focused the world's attention on a city transformed.

The centrepiece City of Manchester Stadium was completed on time and within budget despite persistent and, as it turned out, ill-founded scare stories about structural difficulties. Manchester sported a new, purpose-built Aquatics Centre too; a £22.6 million complex in the heart of the University of Manchester's sprawling campus boasting not only two 50 metre swimming pools, an international-size diving pool and sports science and sports medicine facilities, but also a children's leisure lagoon that ensured that the community would enjoy the legacy of the Commonwealth Games afterwards. The project, completed ten weeks ahead of programme, won the prestigious International Olympic Committee/IAKS Award in 2003 for its exemplary design and operation. And if Manchester had been disappointed that a Metrolink tram line was not opened between the city centre and SportCity for the opening of the games – the link is still unbuilt - at least it could boast the completion of Network Rail's £108 million remodelling of the Piccadilly Station complex, with new concourse, pedestrianised station approach and new entrance from Fairfield Street.

Delivery of the sporting venues and essential infrastructure, however, was only part of the Commonwealth Games' success story. Manchester exuded pride and confidence before an audience of 400,000 visitors to the city and a billion more around the world who watched the spectacle on television. The old, persistent image of Manchester as a grim, decaying industrial relic, a sad shadow of its Victorian prime, was blown away by the sheer verve of the occasion. The city had healed its wounds and emerged from the devastating blow of the IRA's bombing with renewed dynamism. And the Commonwealth Games enabled an international audience to enjoy a close-up view of what had been achieved.

Richard Leese said: "The games provided both an unprecedented opportunity to change the image and perception of the city in the eyes of international investors and visitors, and a world-class platform on which to build regeneration and marketing strategies to realise and promote the potential and success of the city."

The 38,000 spectators packed into the City of Manchester Stadium for the opening ceremony were treated to far more than a fanfare from the police band. The city's perseverance in arguing that a national event required government backing for an impressive and prestigious launch won the day. A 4,000-strong cast delivered a £12 million ceremony of pomp and pop which unfolded over more than two hours. The show began with five-times Olympic rowing champion Sir Steve Redgrave pounding a ceremonial drum; the Grenadier Guards shared the arena with pop stars S Club, and the Queen's arrival to receive the Golden Jubilee Commonwealth Baton – delivered by an acrobat slung from a balloon - was greeted by a fly-past by the RAF's Red Arrows aerobatic team.

If the monarch seemed nonplussed by the appearance of England soccer captain and Manchester's United's superstar player David Beckham in a shimmering white and silver tracksuit, hand in hand with Kirsty Howard, the brave little campaigner for the Francis House Children's Hospice opened by Diana, Princess of Wales, it was a passing moment.

The eruption of fireworks at the finale could be seen from the Pennine hills, 20 miles away. The legacy of the games, like that of the task of rebuilding Manchester city centre, was to be the measure of their success. The hosting of the event was as much about raising the city's profile and capitalising on the massive investment in sporting facilities to spur the regeneration process. Some 5,000 new jobs were created in the process and the army of volunteers who became temporary ambassadors for the city proved a remarkable demonstration of new-found Manchester pride.

The recruitment programme to fill 10,000 voluntary positions for the period of the 2002 Commonwealth Games had been launched a year earlier. Initially there was some concern as to whether it would be possible to fill all the positions as a volunteer programme on this scale was unprecedented in peacetime Britain. Many thought that recruiting 10,000 unpaid workers would prove difficult in a country in which volunteering was not a routine part of the culture. However, these reservations proved to be totally unfounded as there was a tremendous response from the people of Manchester and the North West (around 80 per cent of those whose applications were successful originated from the North West of England).

In total 22,346 people applied for the 10,311 roles, of which 53 per cent were women and 47 per cent men. The oldest volunteer was 87-year-old Desmond Pastore from Northenden, Manchester, who worked as an assistant on the statistics desk at the Rugby Sevens tournament. One of the priorities of the volunteer programme had been to encourage applications from the long-term unemployed, ethnic minorities, people from deprived areas and those with disabilities and special needs. The programme offered training and all the volunteers were issued with a free Games uniform which was designed to be distinctive and easily identifiable.

The purple shell suit and northern-style flat cap attracted a lot of negative comments but the resulting national media attention, combined with the fact that Coronation Street's Norris Cole regularly donned his during the popular TV show, helped to raise awareness of the Games across Britain. The volunteers were most visible when directing spectators around the city centre or acting as stewards for the sports venues, but they were involved in many different aspects of the running of the Games in fields as diverse as logistics, medical services, catering and marketing.

The legacy issue had always been uppermost in the minds of the games organisers. When the City of Manchester Stadium and the Aquatics Centre were completed, there was some criticism that the venues were too small to host future major competitions like the Olympic Games. The tearing up of the running track from the former attracted particularly unfavourable comment. But council leader Richard Leese and his predecessor, Graham Stringer, were adamant that there would be commercial after-use for every venue. They had learned from other cities' multi-sports events for which award-winning venues had been built but later became economic burdens. The City of Manchester Stadium had been declared the new home of Manchester City Football Club before it was ever built and the swimming complex had to fulfil the city's requirement for multi-purpose use.

"We had to make sure that everyone benefited from these investments, not just elite athletes," said Leese. "Every sports venue in Manchester, whatever the standard of the building, has to be one that every resident can use, either as an individual or as part of one of our sports development programmes."

The combination of the transformation of Manchester's city centre and the platform provided by the Commonwealth Games to show it off to the world, paid lucrative dividends. Visitors to the city are adding almost £2 billion a year to Manchester's economy according to a post-Games study commissioned Marketing Manchester. And, as the tenth anniversary of the terrorist bomb approached, the national tourist agency, Visit Britain, nominated Manchester "destination of the month", by quoting the Lonely Planet Guide's view that: "Manchester is one of the few spots on the island that can look London squarely in the eye and say: 'This is how it's done, mate'."

Chapter Eighteen

Boom

TEN years on from the devastating blast in the heart of Manchester – and almost 20 after the astonishing political sea change that enabled it not only to recover from the blow so remarkably, but to set its sights ever higher – the momentum that has carried the city so far has shown no sign of flagging. In 2006, a decade after the IRA primed its fuse, the skyline was dominated by more tower cranes than at any time during the post-bomb reconstruction of the city's shattered core. For nothing breeds success like success. Manchester's recovery is a tangible achievement and what has been accomplished has paved the way for ongoing and future visions.

Ian Simpson, the architect on whose simple ideas the rebuilding Masterplan was based, sees the next ten years in Manchester as being as exciting, if not more so, than the last. The architect of Urbis and One Deansgate commands national and international admiration for his work on new Manchester, but he acknowledges that his firm's dramatic post-bomb success was all about timing.

"We just happened to be around at the time, working in the city, familiar with what was going on. I'd moved up from London to set up a practice in Manchester with Rachael when the bomb went off. I could have been still working in London and had no involvement at all. Then we had one or two ideas that chimed with the aspirations and ambitions of the city and we won the competitions for the Masterplan and Urbis. It was a fantastic springboard for us to start work on really important bits of the city, though we had to work hard for it."

Simpson's slender Hilton Tower – 515 feet to its roof and topped by a 45-

foot spire – eclipses the height of the 400 foot CIS Building which dominated the cityscape for more than 40 years as Manchester's tallest skyscraper. But it is just the first of several new monuments to the city's centre's buoyant economy. The Albany Place development will see a tower rising to 430 feet – another Simpson design – above the long-abandoned Labour Exchange in Aytoun Street. And when the Piccadilly tower, developed by inacity - whose lack of capital letters is more than made up for by lofty ambition - is complete, it will soar to 616 feet, to become the tallest residential skyscraper in Europe.

Simpson said: "What was achieved in Manchester after the bomb was probably the best that could have been achieved in the situation the city found itself. Some plans envisaged the complete demolition of the Arndale Centre, but that could never have happened; it was unaffordable. It would have cost £1.5 billion just to buy out the existing tenant leases – a complete non-starter. But the dynamism of what was done means that the next decade will be at least as exciting as the last. We have a city council and a private sector in a partnership that delivered some very difficult projects in a climate that they largely generated for themselves. The result has been to put Manchester five to ten years ahead of comparative cities like Leeds and Newcastle and the confidence created is very attractive to investment from within Britain and the rest of Europe.

"When I hear people stopping in the street, pointing up to One Deansgate and proudly saying: 'That's where the footballers live,' I think it's just great."

Manchester's ability to reach for the sky and court the 'Wow Factor' with such visible statements is borne out by official statistics that show the city has proportionately outstripped London in terms of economic growth since the IRA detonation. While the document containing the figures, published by the Office of the Deputy Prime Minister, concedes the truth behind northern cities' long-expressed lament – that London gets more than its fair share of national resources – Manchester was singled out as the "notable exception to a pattern of southern cities growing faster than their northern counterparts". Whether the recommended antidote – policies for shifting power and resources from the capital to the regions – will ever overcome Whitehall's endemic London-centric view in the future remains to be seen. It will take a degree of political resolve not yet evident. The economic dominance of London and the South East will probably not be challenged or even challengeable until the overheating and overcrowding there becomes intolerable.

For all Manchester's remarkable recent accomplishments, bucking the trend despite its commercial core being all but destroyed, the task remains an arduous one to create a city where the transformation of the centre is matched by a similar renaissance elsewhere in wider Manchester. In the meantime Manchester can only build on its strengths. The claim to be England's second city is based upon the fact that Manchester generates almost as much economic activity as Leeds, Liverpool and Sheffield combined, and, with the biggest university campus in Europe within a three-mile radius of the city centre, the future of Cottonopolis lies in knowledge-based pursuits involving research contracts in the merged universities, the media and information technology industries.

Between the booming city centre and the affluent suburbs, particularly to the south, remains a ring containing deprivation, poverty, poor health, high unemployment and low educational attainment. The challenge ahead is to deploy in these areas the talent and the techniques that, according to Simpson's calculations, saw the central area leap forward 30 years in the space of just ten following the bomb.

East Manchester has its SportCity and its own urban regeneration company; the rippling out of value from the city centre has begun in earnest. The rebranding of Ancoats, the world's first industrial suburb, as New Islington, is the £240 million vision for a "Millennium, Village" that will span the divide between the prosperous centre and the districts reinventing themselves to the east. The developer is Urban Splash, Tom Bloxham's pioneering company that revolutionised city centre living with its imaginative conversions of former industrial buildings into high-value homes.

There is much still to do. The Director of the London School of Economics, Sir Howard Davies, was born and brought up in the north Manchester district of Blackley and is a regular visitor to his home city. The former Director General of the Confederation of British Industry who also served for two years as Deputy Governor of the Bank of England, said he saw Manchester ten years on from the bomb as "a glass half full". Manchester had definitely lost its reputation for what he described as its "left wing joke" status of the 1980s, and the Commonwealth Games and the regeneration of the bombed out central core had been "real achievements".

"You do get a sense that the city is a more dynamic place after what's happened in Castlefield, with Urbis and the loads of exciting things that have been taking place," he said. "But on the other hand I watched a match at the City of Manchester Stadium between Manchester City and Charlton and decided to walk back to Piccadilly station at about 7pm on a Sunday night. It made me very aware of the work that remains to be done, and how close in it is – between the city centre and that spanking new stadium. There are places of complete dereliction still, which is quite depressing, so while I'm perfectly happy to say Manchester is in a lot better shape than it was and life is a lot more optimistic, there's still huge scope there; still large areas of post-industrial wasteland which have got to be grappled with."

Richard Leese, who passed a personal landmark in the weeks running up the tenth anniversary of the IRA bomb – clocking up a decade as leader of the city council – concurred completely with Davies' qualified approval of Manchester's progress.

"It's true – there's a lot still to do," he admitted. "I think that over the last decade we've dug the foundations. I don't want to understate what has been achieved over the last ten years, but while we have created a position where we are just about growing at the same rate as London and the South East, we are certainly not narrowing the gap as we need to do. Again, while Manchester's performance is well up in terms of European standards, it is not yet comparable with the best in Europe. We are not up there with some German cities and, say, Helsinki, which is where we aim to be."

Leese took encouragement from the major construction projects ongoing in the city centre and the fact that some of the inner city suburbs like Didsbury and Chorlton had not just become desirable places to live in themselves, but their success was spilling into neighbouring areas like Whalley Range and Levenshulme. Beswick, which might once have laid claim to being the most deprived district of east Manchester, and therefore the country, had seen a real transformation; but the scale of the regeneration task across the area as a whole dictated a lengthy timeframe. When the city developed its east Manchester regeneration strategy, officials calculated that if all the right ingredients were in place it would involve a 20-year programme. "We're about five years in," said Leese in the spring of 2006. "We've done pretty well but there are still fifteen years of our timetable to go."

A recipe for success contained in the government's State of the Cities Report, launched in March 2006 by the Office of the Deputy Prime Minister, reflected the elements that had contributed to Manchester's progress over the last two decades: stability and leadership, new people and new ideas. Local Government minister David Milibrand named names; Leese, Sir Howard Bernstein and others had provided just such leadership, but also a management style that encouraged ideas and thinking. This had been the context within which local entrepreneurs like Tom Bloxham and fellow property developers, Carol Ainscow and Stuart Wall, had built their businesses and were important elements in taking the city forward.

Manchester's leading designers and entrepreneurs, who made their reputations in the city centre, are now engaged in development projects for whole areas. Public-private partnerships of the kind tried and tested in Manchester again and again are clearly seen as the way forward. Said Leese: "One of the things that's unique about Manchester's economic revival, compared with virtually everywhere else in the UK, is that here it is disproportionately private sector led. And I think that is a good thing."

However far Leese and his colleagues may have travelled since the mid-1980s when they were perceived as being unwilling to work with the private sector at all, the top of his political agenda two decades later would have been, however, very familiar to the left wing zealots who took control of Manchester in 1984. In a word, jobs.

"It's great having all these new jobs coming to the city centre, though getting the jobs does not guarantee local benefit," he said. "On the other hand, not creating jobs means there cannot be any local benefit at all. So as well as attracting employment, one of the biggest tasks we still face in some parts of the city is raising skills and aspirations in order for people to benefit from what's going on. Upskilling the people of Manchester is vital and I feel more confident than I have for the last five years that in the next five we'll have the tools in place to do that job."

It is deeply ironic that the confrontational nature of British politics causes a failure to acknowledge, in public at least, the cross-party co-operation and "can-do" attitude that Manchester's leaders adopted to drive the city forward. When, as the tenth anniversary of the Manchester bomb approached, the Conservatives launched their Inner Cities task force, headed by none other than Lord Heseltine himself, the rhetoric paid no heed to the reality of the preceding two decades.

David Cameron, the Conservative leader, who accompanied Heseltine to Liverpool for the policy launch, claimed that "too many of Britain's urban areas had been left behind by Labour and let down by complicated and contradictory bureaucratic schemes." The yah-boo riposte from local government minister Milibrand was typically blinkered, claiming that the task force was in the hands of people responsible for "past Tory failures".

The truth as far as Manchester is concerned has been very different since the great policy switch of 1988, as Heseltine is willing to concede. For him, the return to Merseyside was the squaring of a circle begun with the establishment of the Stockbridge Village Trust in the "bombed out" Cantril Farm housing estate in 1979, the first voluntary partnership between what was then a new Conservative government and a Labour council. It had come in the wake of what Heseltine described later as a simple but fundamental change to the allocation of top-up urban grants to local councils to tackle stressed areas.

Back to the future at ground zero

Business as usual in the city centre

"In essence we told them that before they got the money they had to consult with the private sector and come up with proposals as to how they could help augment the public money involved. That is where the principle of public-private partnership really took off. This was the cultural background into which the Labour Party was dragged, kicking and screaming, but my view was quite simple: 'You don't want to work with us? Fine. Good luck. Goodbye. We'll go somewhere where they do'.

"I don't remember any local authority that actually said that their principles were such that they couldn't work with us. They all did and of course they got to know the private sector and suddenly realised that people in the private sector weren't the demons they'd always talked about – and vice versa. The barriers came down and in the end it was all due to personal relationships."

Manchester had learned fast. Heseltine's idea of competitive bidding had come as a culture shock but the former Deputy Prime Minister said: "I happen to believe that the Manchester City Challenge in Hulme was the most exciting of all the urban developments I did. It was big, it was about people, it was in response to a scandal and it was done in co-operation with a very impressive Labour council. They worked very effectively to make City Challenge work. Hulme is today unrecognisable from what it was."

Under Sir Alan Cockshaw, the Hulme initiative had laid the basis for future partnership schemes which Heseltine considered very impressive and which had proved a valuable prelude to the city's response to the bomb.

Heseltine is gratified with the way Manchester's Labour leaders "got on with it". They organised the international design competition and adopted a City Challenge-type approach; he provided the money and the private sector co-operated fully to the extent that the regeneration of the city centre spilled out into areas not originally envisaged.

Looking back ten years after the event – irrespective of party political rhetoric, Heseltine said: "I actually believe that Manchester, once they got used to the idea of working with a Tory government, carried it through effectively and honoured their undertakings. The man I would have heard from had they not done so was Sir Alan Cockshaw. Here was a very senior and experienced industrialist and the city worked very closely with him. I never heard him complain.

"I think it went extremely well. They took the Hulme estate team and transplanted it into the city centre. They had the people, they had the experience and they had the human relationships."

Ten years after the IRA bombed Manchester, the threat of terrorism looms darker than ever over Britain's major cities. Leaders both in government and of the security services have admitted that further attacks are "inevitable" and the suicide bombings on London Transport tube trains and a bus on July 7th, 2005 tragically bore out their fears. The nation not only requires vigilance and preventative measures in place to meet the threat, but also a formula for responding to attacks that are carried out. Manchester's experience provides a valuable template for the future and the Home Office included many of the lessons learned in its official case study, *Business As Usual; a manual for recovery*. Heseltine, who was close to Manchester Millennium Limited when it was first established, said he was looking at all the options Manchester deployed for the Conservatives' regeneration strategy.

Sir Howard Bernstein is clear in his own mind what he considered to be the most important element in Manchester's remarkable recovery, the task force that was assembled within days of the devastating shock of the detonation. "What that demonstrated was how a small, experienced and skilled group of people seconded from the public and private sectors, working to an inclusive board, could provide the energy and the essential co-ordinating role required to drive the city forward. It did both these things in terms of dealing with the immediate aftermath of the bomb and delivering the renewal programme. It didn't represent a constitutional threat to any of the partners involved such as the council, the highways and planning authority, or individual landowners, because we had no compulsory purchase powers.

"It was a very inclusive process which, so long as we were all pursuing shared values and objectives, was able to deliver. It was a Mancunian model. As to whether what we did would work anywhere else is open to question because it all comes down to leadership. It worked for us."

In 1996 Canon Paul Denby, sub-Dean of Manchester Cathedral, helped clear up the wreckage of the windows and clerestories blown out of the great church's south side. Ten years on he reflected how this catastrophe had created a tangible bond within the community.

"The bomb enabled people to feel that they belonged and that the city belonged to them. Pride in Manchester grew and is still growing. And, as we see all the developments around us, each of them, I think, stands as a tribute to the new way forward. We can look ahead with honour, with pride and with hope.

"We have something worthwhile to offer to everyone in the world; the world just needs to come and see us."

The Brown Court entrance of the new Arndale Centre

TESTIMONIALS
FOR
MANCHESTER

**Sir Alex Ferguson, CBE, manager of
Manchester United
April 2006**

"I have been associated with Manchester for nearly twenty years and the transformation of the city in that time has been remarkable. I remember the day of the bombing vividly; Old Trafford was one of the main venues for Euro '96. The spirit and determination of the people of the city to carry on and come back stronger from that blow was inspirational. Manchester – like Old Trafford – has just got better and better. It's a world class city."

Deputy Prime Minister John Prescott
Labour Party Spring conference,
Manchester city centre
April 2004

"The reality of terror explains the heavy security around this conference. It is just eight years ago that Manchester suffered a terrorist attack. But Manchester recovered. The people stood united. Together they built a new city centre. There was triumph in a place of tragedy. The city we see today is vibrant and successful: a testimony to people's courage and defiance in the face of terror."

Andrew Spinoza, Chair of Manchester University Alumni Association and Managing Director of SKV Communications. March 2006

"Before the bomb, we were another European city thinking we could be a major European city. Now we're a major European city with our sights on becoming a major world city."

Sir James Anderton, Chief Constable of Greater Manchester –1974-1992
March 2006

"The entire recorded history of the city of Manchester is an inspirational predication of the indomitable spirit and great fortitude invariably displayed in any given period by the people who live, work and conduct their business within its borders.

The city's capacity to recover, reform and rebuild in times of almost paralysing adversity has been sorely tested on many occasions, not least the aftermath of the Blitz in 1940; but in every case the city has found the wherewithal to restore and strengthen its pride and self-belief.

The terrible events of June 15, 1996 shattered the buildings but not the confidence, nor the abiding mettle of the people of Manchester. Not for the first time, its prescient leaders and steadfast citizens seized the unexpected opportunity to renew, modernize and invigorate the heart of the city, and they have done so with remarkable success.

Enterprising, dedicated men and women have thoughtfully and imaginatively preserved the old with the new, the historic and traditional with the innovative in a way that would surely have pleased our Victorian forebears and will doubtless gladden our present, cosmopolitan, culturally diverse generation.

The result is a hugely impressive, vibrant and attractive, world-renowned city, on the way to an even better and brighter future, and we are greatly indebted to all those involved in this renaissance."

John Monks, General Secretary of the Trades Union Congress 1993-2003, and Mancunian. April 2006.

"To a son of the city, as I am, the renaissance of Manchester since 1996 has been a wonder to behold. The city has never looked brighter or more interesting. People are moving into the city centre having fled from it during the previous 50 years and at its best there is a civilised, friendly buzz.

There is still a way to go before it can be regarded as a great city in Europe but it is going quickly in the right direction and congratulations to all concerned."

Tom Bloxham, MBE, Managing Director, Urban Splash, chairman Arts Council England (North West), Government property advisor. March 2006

"For me the turning point for Manchester came before the bomb and before the Commonwealth Games. It was the second Olympic Games bid when we lost but the city suddenly had a realisation. There was a huge party in Castlefield and people grasped the idea that Manchester should no longer consider itself in competition with the likes of Barnsley and Stockport. It was now up against Barcelona, Los Angeles and Sydney and its aspirations increased accordingly.

The city was further helped by the manner in which politics had moved on from the days of the 'Looney Left' and the canny likes of Graham Stringer, Richard Leese and Howard Bernstein were getting things done.

The music scene was big, there was a cultural renaissance and young entrepreneurs like me found ourselves drawn to Manchester, needing office space, retail space and living space. I am proud Urban Splash played a part in all of what has happened since."

**Michael Heseltine, (now Lord Heseltine)
former Deputy Prime Minister
March 2006**

"Coming to Manchester [after the bombing] was a journey I shall never forget. I sat on the train obviously deeply shocked and horrified. I knew that questions would be asked about what we were going to do; what is the right solution. Then I knew what the right solution was – to see this event, horrific as it was, as an opportunity and, no mucking about, we must do things on the grand scale and to the best quality we can."

John Stalker, writer, broadcaster and former Deputy Chief Constable of Greater Manchester Police:

"Every time I drive into my home city I never cease to marvel at the astonishing changes that have taken place in the last ten years. What has been achieved is quite phenomenal.

"Manchester was my place of work before the bomb and after it and it's like two completely different places. It was a brave decision to build a city for the 21st Century instead of just patching up the damage and the result is a place of wonderment."

The Rt Hon Sir John Major KG CH, Prime Minister, 1990-1997 February 2006

"I have a clear recollection of the IRA bomb in Manchester and the extraordinary response from the city. Although there was, of course, shock, I saw no sign of panic, simply a swift determination to move on and replace what was lost with something better.

It must have been dispiriting for the terrorists to realise that, although they could destroy property – thankfully, on this occasion, not life – they could not destroy willpower, nor gain any advantage from their violence.

I remember feeling enormously proud of Manchester and its model response to an event that could have clouded its future – but was never permitted to do so.

[Mr King's] book is a worthwhile memorial to a catastrophe that showed Manchester at its very best and I send all my good wishes for its success."

15/06/96   53°29.470' N   054° H 202°14.440 K U   10:17:04

The police helicopter monitored the Ford Cargo for an hour before its video
equipment caught the awesome moment of detonation

A quarter of a second later the huge mushroom cloud dwarfed the
Arndale tower block as debris was hurled a mile into the sky